Technology Driven Curriculum for 21st Century Higher Education Students in Africa

Edited by
Lawrence Meda &
Alfred H. Makura

Langaa Research & Publishing CIG
Mankon, Bamenda

Publisher:
Langaa RPCIG
Langaa Research & Publishing Common Initiative Group
P.O. Box 902 Mankon
Bamenda
North West Region
Cameroon
Langaagrp@gmail.com
www.langaa-rpcig.net

Distributed in and outside N. America by African Books Collective
orders@africanbookscollective.com
www.africanbookscollective.com

ISBN-10: 9956-762-47-4

ISBN-13: 978-9956-762-47-7

© Lawrence Meda and Alfred H. Makura 2017

All rights reserved.
No part of this book may be reproduced or transmitted in any form or by any means, mechanical or electronic, including photocopying and recording, or be stored in any information storage or retrieval system, without written permission from the publisher

List of Contributors

Dr. Sekitla Daniel Makhasane holds a PhD in Education Leadership and Management. He worked in some Lesotho schools as a teacher and Deputy Principal. While pursuing postgraduate studies at the University of KwaZulu-Natal, he was also a part-time lecturer in the same university teaching various courses. He is currently a postdoctoral research fellow at the University of KwaZulu-Natal in the Republic of South Africa. His research interests are in the areas of school financial management, education leadership, school violence and ICTs in education.

Alfred H. Makura is an Assoiate Professor in the Faculty of Humanities at Central University of Technology, Free State, Bloemfontein campus, Department of Postgraduate Studies (Education) offering Education Law and Research. Initially, Prof Makura worked briefly as a high school teacher (in Swaziland, Lesotho & Zimbabwe) and extensively as lecturer at Morgenster Teachers' College, an Associate College of the University of Zimbabwe, and at the Zimbabwe Open University. Prof Makura also worked as Senior Consultant at the University of Fort Hare's Teaching and Learning Centre for five years prior to his current posting. He holds a PhD(Education); a Post Graduate Dilploma in Higher Education and Training; a Certificate in the Facilitation of Learning; a Master of Education (in Education Leadership & Management); a B. A. Education and a Diploma in Agricultural Education. To date, Prof Makura has to his credit: published two books, 2 book chapters and at least twenty five peer reviewed journal articles. He has presented no less than 30 papers at local and international conferences. His areas of speciality and interest are education, education leadership and management, curriculum development, gender and teacher professional development in higher education. He is passionate about issues of female leadership and teacher education in general. He is a keen and passionate reader and a music and soccer lover.

Mr. Raymond Nkwenti Fru is a Cameroonian national. He lectures History Education in the Faculty of Education at the National University of Lesotho. He holds the following academic qualifications: Diploma of Education from the Higher Teachers Training College Annex of the University of Yaounde 1; Bachelor of Education (B.Ed. Honours) and Masters of Education (M.Ed.) Degrees from the University of KwaZulu-Natal in South Africa, specialising in History Education. He is in the process of finalising a Ph.D. with the same institution (University of KwaZulu-Natal). His research interests are in textbook representations and general education issues with particular focus on History Education.

Dr. Fanny Saruchera is a Senior Lecturer, researcher, consultant and a reviewer. He is currently stationed at Namibia University of Science & Technology (NUST), formerly Polytechnic of Namibia in the Faculty of Management Sciences servicing the departments of Marketing & Logistics, Graduate School of Business as well as the Namibian-German Centre for Logistics. His research interests include inter-disciplinary studies, transport and logistics, consumer mythology and other related themes.

Dr Africa Makasi is an accomplished University Lecturer and business consultant with over 10 years University lectureship experience. His publication interests are in e-marketing, disruptive innovation, consumer behaviour and service quality. His prowess in marketing is enhanced by an impeccable practical working experience in the public and private sectors for which he has worked at senior management level. He is a holder of a Bachelor of Business Administration Degree (Marketing), Masters of Science Degree in Marketing (NUST, Zim), and PhD in Marketing (UKZN, RSA).

Dr. Remmy Shiundu Barasa has vast experience in teaching literature and English language at both public and private universities in Kenya and Tanzania. He currently teaches at Pwani University in Kenya. Dr. Shiundu has interests in postcolonial literature, culture and gender. He has co-authored Tales, Tellers and Tale-Making: A Critical Study of Literary Stylistics and Narrative Styles in Contemporary African Literature (2010), among other literary essays.

Dr. Lawrence Meda holds a PhD in Education (Curriculum Studies) from the University of KwaZulu Natal in South Africa. He is currently working at Cape Peninsula University of Technology as a Senior Lecturer and Teaching and Learning Coordinator in the Faculty of Education. His research interests are in Curriculum Studies; Inclusive Education; Teacher Education and Technology in Education.

Dr. Silas Parowa Mangwende is a distinguished lecturer in the Faculty of Management and Entrepreneurial Development Studies at the Women's University in Africa, Harare, Zimbabwe. He is an expert in Financial Mathematics and Statistics with over 10 years' experience in university teaching. He is a member of the University Higher Degrees Committee, Research Board and Senate. Dr Mangwende is interested in interdisciplinary research in which he applies mathematical and statistical models to get insight into phenomena. His recent researches focus on Mathematics and Higher Education Curriculum as well as Technology and Higher Education Curriculum. He was awarded the Vice Chancellor Best Lecturer of the Year 2015 through his outstanding teaching skills. His doctoral thesis is characterised by the development of out-of-school entrepreneurship model using mathematical functional relationships.

Ms. Bernadatte Namirembe is a Ugandan and teacher by profession. She was working as an Assistant Lecturer at St Augustine University of Tanzania in its constituent college of Tabora (Archbishop Mihayo University College of Tabora- AMUCTA) until October 2016. Currently, she is back to Uganda and is at the initial stages of developing her PhD proposal in Deaf Education. She has a Master Degree in Educational Foundations from the Makerere University - Uganda (2007) and a Bachelor of Arts with Education Degree Makerere University (1997). She has been specializing in deaf education and she has trained both specialised teachers of the deaf and regular teachers. She has coordinated an international exchange project with Royal Dutch Kentalis, from the Netherlands, financed by American Philanthropy (PSIPSE) "Teaching Deaf Learners – A pilot on innovative teaching skills in Tanzania" (2014 -2016) which was implemented at AMUCTA. She has coordinated Special

Education from 2013 – 2015 and worked as Head of Educational Foundations Department (2011 – 2013) at AMUCTA. She has also participated in research and conferences, for example the ICED 2015 in Greece where she presented a paper on teaching of deaf learners in Tanzania.

Mr. Ezra Nathanael Ntazoya holds a Masters of Arts in Education (M.A Ed) from University of Dar es Salaam-Tanzania. He also holds a Postgraduate Diploma in Procurement and Supply Management from the College of Business Education-Dar es Salaam Campus-Tanzania. He is currently an Assistant Lecturer and Head of Department – Educational Foundations at Archbishop Mihayo University College of Tabora (AMUCTA). His areas of interests in teaching and research are Curriculum (Teaching and Learning), Educational Media and Technology, Assessment and Evaluation at Higher Learning and Psychology of learning. He has taught Geography and History in secondary schools for eight years. He is currently teaching Introduction to Educational Psychology, Curriculum Development and Evaluation in undergraduate to postgraduate levels. He also teaches Certificate and Diploma courses in the Department of Business Administration.

Dr. Louis Okon Akpan is a Nigerian and married with three girls. His academic journey started about 20 years ago. In 1995, he obtained B.Sc. (Ed.) in Geography/Education from the University of Calabar. On graduation, he proceeded to the University of Ibadan for the M.Sc. in Climatology in 2001. He graduated with another Masters' degree in Comparative Education at the same university in 2003. He obtained Ph.D. in 2016 from the University of KwaZulu-Natal, South Africa. His research interests in the past twelve years have been directed essentially towards the teaching of History and Policy of Education, Comparative Education, Nomadic Education in Nigeria and Aboriginal Education in Australia. He has publications in some renowned journals and book chapters. Currently, he is an assistant director in an education research institution in Uyo, Nigeria.

Table of Contents

Chapter 1: Introduction - Towards a technology driven curriculum.................................. 1
Lawrence Meda

Chapter 2: Students' views on integrating technology in learning at a University in Lesotho............ 5
Sekitla Daniel Makhasane and Raymond Nkwenti Fru

Chapter 3: Prior access to modern learning technologies as a predictor of Post-Admission Cognitive Dissonance in African universities: Evidence from Namibia and Zimbabwe................................... 27
Fanny Saruchera and Africa Makasi

Chapter 4: Effectiveness of digital technology in teaching of literature in Kenyan universities: A case study of Pwani University............................... 51
Remmy Shiundu Barasa

Chapter 5: Postgraduate Certificate in Education students' perspectives about learning using Blackboard at a university in South Africa....................................... 79
Lawrence Meda

Chapter 6: Student use of technology
in Higher Education in Zimbabwe..............................101
   Silas Parowa Mangwende

Chapter 7: Teaching pre-service teachers
to integrate technology for inclusive
classrooms with deaf learners in Tanzania.....................127
   Bernadatte Namirembe

Chapter 8: Using technology to assess
students at a university in Tanzania:
Lecturers' perspectives..161
   Ezra Nathanael Ntazoya

Chapter 9: University education and
its impact on Nigerian technological
advancement..187
   Louis Okon Akpan

Chapter 10: Conclusion - Envisioning
technology driven curriculum in
African Higher Education: Ubuntu perspective...............213
   Sekitla Daniel Makhasane and Lawrence Meda

Chapter 1

Introduction: Towards a Technology Driven Curriculum

Lawrence Meda

In this contemporary digital era, educational technology is playing an increasingly important role. It has become so ubiquitous and fundamental in teaching and learning in higher education. Students of the 21st-century desire opportunities to learn in real time, anytime, and on their own terms using technology. This challenges lecturers in institutions of higher learning to be creative and innovative in curriculum design and pedagogy, in order to meet the needs and expectations of students in the digital era.

A good curriculum is one that is not just responsive to the needs of students but also to what is happening in the environment at the time. The use of digital strategies and space is what is happening in the higher education environment today, hence, a need for curriculum design and pedagogy to enhance this initiative. There is a need for curriculum design and pedagogy to be responsive to the use of technology in learning in a higher education African context.

This book presents research in the area of higher education curriculum and technology in seven African countries. It touches upon the following sub-themes:

- Implications of the integration of technology in the curriculum
  - Curriculum development in the digital era
  - Student perspectives on learning using technology
  - Staff perspectives on teaching using technology
  - Instructional technology across different subjects / courses
  - Assessment and technology
  - Gender and technology in the curriculum
  - Technology and disability: A challenge?
  - Social media and curriculum

- Technology education

The book came about as a result of a call for chapters which was sent to lecturers in numerous African universities. The call for chapters was not restrictive, but open to all lecturers involved in using technology in curriculum design and implementation. Prior to writing full chapters, authors were requested to submit short proposals outlining how their manuscripts relate to the central theme and sub-themes of the book. They were 12 authors from 12 different African universities who sent short proposals. All proposals were scrutinised by the editors and sent back with detailed comments. Four authors could not continue with the project of writing full chapters. Remaining authors wrote eight chapters which cover data relative to the use of educational technologies in higher education in six countries of East and Southern Africa plus a literature review relative to Nigeria in West Africa. Each of the chapters in this book was reviewed by both editors and sent back to authors for revision. Soon thereafter, the chapters were submitted to Langaa Academic Publishers where they were peer reviewed. Each author revised his/her chapter in accordance with reviewers' comments and resubmitted to editors who reviewed the work and eventually submitted to the publisher.

Makhasane and Fru set the stage by discussing students' views on integrating technology into learning at a university in Lesotho. The findings show that students actively collaborated and shared knowledge with one another through the use of formal and informal ICT platforms amidst a shortage of resources. They used informal platforms such as Facebook and WhatsApp more than formal platforms. The authors conclude that in a situation where university ICT resources and infrastructures are scarce, students will rely on the use of easily accessible digital gadgets.

Saruchera and Makasi focus on two African countries – Zimbabwe and Namibia. They investigated the effect of prior access to modern learning technologies as a predictor of post-admission cognitive dissonance (PACD) and the subsequent implications on students' performance. It was found that over 80% of students who had no access to technology displayed high levels of post enrolment dissonance. Over 89% of students who lacked prior access to technology were performing below average, while some did not even bother to do their assigned work primarily due to lack of technical knowledge.

Barasa looked at the effectiveness of digital technology in the teaching of literature at Pwani University in Kenya. The study found that students are increasingly using digital technologies for more effective learning of literature. Students are keen to learn using technology and devices which they already have in their possession. The author makes policy recommendations, for example, university senates should approve and fast track digital learning policies. The government should give budgetary allocations to e-learning in the universities to target improvement of digital infrastructure, research, capacity building, and attitude management and create awareness. To lecturers, the author recommended that they should be motivated and trained to use e-learning in their subject areas in a more interactive and effective way.

Meda focused on Postgraduate Certificate in Education (PGCE) students' perspectives about learning using Blackboard at a university in South Africa. He found that although students are debilitated by poor internet connectivity on campus, they are enthusiastic about learning using the platform. He concluded that Blackboard suits the context of PGCE students and responds to their needs and expectations of learning in the 21st century.

Mangwende examined the use of technology by students in a higher education context in Zimbabwe. He found that students use internet for both academic and non-academic purposes. When the internet was utilised for academic purposes, it was for searching for learning and research material. It was also established that students minimally used the websites for learning purposes.

Namirembe investigated the teaching of pre-service teachers to integrate technology to differentiate pedagogical practices for inclusive classrooms with deaf learners in Tanzania. The study provides an insight on how teachers in developing countries can be trained to integrate technology in pedagogy. The findings suggest that the DI model can be used to train pre-service teachers to use technology in teaching if they have poor computer background.

Ntazoya also focused on the Tanzanian context. He explored the use of technology in assessing university students. Findings indicate that lecturers for the most part assess students using the prescribed assessment techniques without necessarily integrating technology. Results also revealed that, both lecturers and students need training on the applicability of various computer based skills essential for assessment process. The author recommends that assessment techniques used by instructors should be aligned to the current trends on technology and major innovations that could help both the instructors and students to do better in their teaching and learning endeavourers respectively.

Finally, Akpan explores the impact university education has on Nigeria's technological advancement and demonstrates how science and technology education impact the Nigerian economy in the areas of agriculture, oil and gas, solid minerals and mining, and manufacturing.

Chapter 2

Students' views on integrating technology in learning at a University in Lesotho

Sekitla Daniel Makhasane
&
Raymond Nkwenti Fru

Abstract

Universities throughout the world are tapping into the benefits of integrating ICTs into teaching and learning. Many studies have since focused on how ICTs are used for teaching in the universities. This chapter reports the views and perspectives of students in one Lesotho University regarding their integration of ICTs into learning. The chapter employs a qualitative approach involving data generated through interviews with six students purposely selected across university faculties. The findings suggest that students actively collaborated and shared knowledge with one another through the use of formal and informal ICTs' platforms amidst a shortage of resources. These platforms were at times confronted with contradictions regarding the intended and the actual use. The findings further revealed that students used informal platforms such as Facebook and WhatsApp more than formal platforms. We consequently argue that in a situation where University ICT resources and infrastructures, are scarce students will rely on the use of easily accessible ICTs' resources. We recommend that informal platforms be integrated into teaching and learning by university academics.

Keywords: ICTs, learning, informal, formal, higher education

Introduction and Background

The 21st century has witnessed a paradigm shift in higher education institutions throughout the world as a result of the integration of Information and Communication Technologies (ICTs) into teaching and learning (Vajargan, Jahani & Azadman, 2010). In the 21st century, students learn better through ICTs (Joo, Kim & Kim, 2016). Thang, Lee, Murugaiah, Jaafar, Tan and Bukhari (2016) found that students value the integration of ICTs into teaching and learning, but they used them more for social than educational purposes.

There is an emerging literature which attests that institutions of higher learning in many countries have positioned ICTs as a priority on the education agenda. The use of social media, for example, in teaching and learning seems to be a new catch to researchers since it is relatively new and evolving (Gikas & Grant, 2013). In the era of the knowledge society, ICTs play a central role hence the need to incorporate them in university education (Maphosa & Mudzielwana, 2014). Lesotho is no exception in this regard. At the policy level, the Lesotho government recognises the importance of ICTs for socio-economic development through the adoption of ICTs' policy in 2005. This policy sets out clear objectives for human resources development and education. In particular, the policy commits the government in collaboration with the private sector to invest in education for, inter alia, ICTs' financing. In addition, educational institutions are called upon to create infrastructures necessary for ICTs (Lesotho Ministry of Communications, Science and Technology, 2005). However, the Lesotho Higher Education Policy highlights challenges underpinning integration of ICTs into teaching and learning. Such challenges include lack of essential infrastructures such as computers, limited Internet and intranet capacity and the unwillingness of staff members to adopt new teaching approaches using ICTs (Lesotho Government, 2013). Against this backdrop, it is essential to explore the views of students pertaining to the use of ICTs in learning.

There is a growing interest in researching social media as communication channels used by students in higher learning institutions. Social media, web 2.0 and social software are terms used interchangeably in the 21st century in reference to technologies which use the internet as a platform for social relations aimed at collaboration, communication and creative expression (Dabbagh & Kitsantas, 2012). Many students from all walks of life have a great passion for using social media regardless of their geographical area (Taleba & Sohrabib, 2012). Thus, the process of learning is influenced by technology in general and social media in particular. Through social media platforms, students are able to connect and share information with many people from different parts of the world. In this way, learning through social media can be regarded as social, interactive and constructivist (Joo et al, 2016). Examples of social media that students can use for learning include Twitter, Facebook, friend wise, flicker, friendster, Instagram, Youtube, storify, hashtags, Google hangouts, second life and Edmodo (Joo et al, 2016; Thang et al, 2016).

Valentín, Mateos, González-Tablas, Pérez, López and García (2013) found that university students' use of different ICTs ranges from more use of some technologies to lesser use of others. Further, students used ICTs for four main reasons namely: social use, technical use, academic use and educational platform use. Examples of social use include chats and forums while technical use focuses on web page design, data management programmes and audiovisual programmes. Academic use portrays the utilisation of office programmes identified with academic tasks, for example, the presentation and elaboration activities (word processors, power point presentations and so forth). Educational platform use depicts the utilisation of the technologies made available by the universities to provide students with essential resources that will enable them to achieve the competencies required in the courses they follow.

Statement of the problem

ICTs are widely used in socioeconomic and political sectors of societies throughout the world. Literature pertaining to the need for usage of ICTs in education is burgeoning. Of particular interest to the current study, is the great concern for integration of ICTs into teaching and learning in the universities. Despite an enabling policy framework which favours such integration, in practice, the opposite prevails. As highlighted earlier Lesotho's policy framework illustrates a political will towards the use of ICTs in institutions of higher learning. Be that as it may, literature alludes to various challenges of integrating ICTs into teaching and learning. Wallet (2015), for example, paints a picture of multiple challenges regarding the use of ICTs in many countries found in the Sub-Saharan region. Such challenges include, inter alia, lack of financial resources, shortage of competent human resources and absence of basic infrastructure. It is worth noting that universities in the developing world are mostly affected by these challenges. Lesotho is one of the countries located in the developing world and therefore is faced with myriad challenges as far as ICTs are concerned. The literature on the integration of ICTs into teaching and learning in higher education seems to be dominated by that which can be done by lecturers as facilitators of teaching and learning (Adams, 2003; Hardman, 2005; Maoba, 2009). Little is known about how students use ICTs in learning. This chapter focuses on adding knowledge in that regard.

Theoretical framework

Activity theory is adopted to frame this chapter. According to Bellamy (2001), activity theory was developed by Leont'ev who based it on the work of Vygosky (1978). It was later extended by Cole and Engerstrom. This theory emphasises the importance of technology as an essential tool for mediation of human action (Bodker, 2001; Hashim & Jones, 2007). In order to make sense of an activity, one needs to consider the manner in which artefacts such as ICTs mediate such activity in a given cultural context. It is assumed that the artefacts mediate between the subject and the object. In this chapter, the subject refers to the students and the object denotes the learning purpose. In pursuit of an activity, the subject functions as part of the community. In this sense, it frames learning as constituting of these elements: object (the activity), subject, mediating artefacts (Isssroff & Scanlon, 2002), rules, community and division of labour (Kuutti 2001; McMillan, 2009). Within the structure of activity theory, there are relationships between the components. The tools mediate the relationships between the object and the subject while the rules mediate the relationship between the community and the subject. The rules can either be implicit or explicit conventions, norms and social relations in a given community (Isssroff & Scanlon, 2002).

Here the activity of students' learning is used as a unit of analysis (Hardman, 2005). As stated above, the analytical concepts of this activity involve students and various ICTs that they use for learning as well as rules they have to observe as members of the university community. Thus, activity theory was appropriate as a theoretical base for unpacking experiences, perspectives and views of students pertaining to the manner in which they use ICTs for learning.

Purpose of the study

The purpose of this chapter is to explore the views of students at a university in Lesotho regarding integration of ICTs into learning.

Significance of the study

This chapter intends to contribute knowledge on the perspectives of university students pertaining to their use of ICTs in learning. The knowledge is of paramount importance in the 21st century where ICTs have revolutionised teaching and learning in the universities. Policy makers and practitioners are likely to benefit from this study. In order to formulate appropriate policies, decision makers require information about the manner in which students use and perceive integration of ICTs into learning. At a macro level (Government) decision makers may require information regarding implementation of the policies they formulated. Specifically, for this study, the Lesotho Government has an ICT policy in place which among other issues, has mandated universities to make available resources necessary for use of ICTs (Lesotho Ministry of Communications, Science and Technology, 2005). This study is, therefore, relevant as a potential benchmark of students' views of the nature and usefulness of available ICT infrastructures and resources at one Lesotho University. This view can be extended further to indicate that policy makers in other countries may also benefit from this study. While the findings in this chapter may not necessarily be applicable to all situations, policy makers in a similar context may draw some lessons. At a micro level (university), the findings from this study have the potential to benefit university management, lecturers, students and other members of the university community.

Key research questions

This chapter is guided by the following key research questions:
- What are students' views of integrating ICTs into learning in one Lesotho University?
- How do students in one Lesotho University integrate ICTs into their learning?

Methodology

This section presents the methodology which was adopted in order to address the research questions and problem in this study. This being an empirical study that sought to examine the views and perspectives of students with regard to the use and integration of ICTs into learning in a Lesotho university, the research was done using the constructivist-interpretive paradigm (Danzin & Lincoln, 2005). This paradigm was chosen because it allows researchers to view and understand the socially constructed realities of the participants (De vos et al., 2005) with regard to their interaction with educational technologies. The study, therefore, produced descriptive analysis that emphasises deep interpretive understanding of students' interaction with the social phenomenon of ICT and learning (Henning, 2004). The paradigmatic premise for this study is that the understanding of the experiences of students on using ICT are socially constructed rather than given since ICTs are socially constructed tools for learning. Therefore, the phenomenon of ICT in this study was understood through the meanings (social constructions, consciousness or shared meanings) that the students assigned to them (Nieuwenhuis, 2007).

In line with the constructivist paradigm explained above, this study is also aligned with a qualitative approach since we sought a comprehensive understanding of the views of students regarding learning using ICTs. As a result, it was essential to visit the participants and grant them an opportunity to tell their stories, views and perspectives (Creswell, 2014).

The selection of the sample for this study took the following aspects into consideration: We did not consider students in the first year of study because they would not have gathered enough experiences on the use of ICT due to their limited time spent at the university. Moreover, we selected students from different faculties and programmes to have a diversity of experiences from across the spectrum of the university. Lastly, the sample also involved a mixture of gender representation to mitigate the possibility of ICT experiences being linked to gender roles. Consequently, the population considered for this study involved all students at the university in question enrolled for the second to the fourth year of study. Therefore, the purposive sampling technique was applied to select the six participants who constituted the sample for this study due to our judgement that these participants comprised elements that contain the most characteristics, representative or typical attributes of the population under consideration (Cohen et al., 2011; Strydom & Venter, 2004). Being a qualitative study, Cohen et al. (2007, p.115) remind us that the sample does not have to be representative or generalisable, rather "the concern is to acquire in-depth information from those who are in a position to give it". There was no consideration of gender in the selection of the participants for this study, however, by fate rather than design; we ended up with a gender ratio of 4:2 for male and female respectively. The participants were selected from the different faculties of the university with three from Education, two from the Humanities and one from the Faculty of Social Sciences. The rationale for selecting across faculties was to have a wide range also test if some ICT-related experiences from the students were faculty related.

The data was gathered through a process of semi-structured interviews that involved a set of predetermined questions, allowing for probing and clarification of answers around a schedule that basically defined the line of our enquiry (Nieuwenhuis, 2007). In line with the qualitative research tradition, we made sure to listen very attentively to the responses of the participants so that we could "identify new emerging lines of inquiry that are directly related to the phenomenon being studied, and explore and probe these" (Nieuwenhuis, 2007, p. 87). This we did whilst making sure not to get sidetracked by trivial issues that are not related to the study. A tape recorder was used to record the interviews, with the permission of the participants. Meanwhile, notes were also taken simultaneously with the tape recording so that the answers could be reviewed at the end of the interview or to facilitate the process of probing that was used to obtain the maximum amount of data or to ensure that what we had heard was exactly what the participant had meant. The recorded data collected from the interviews was then transcribed and open coded to reveal the themes, trends and patterns that emerged in line with procedures for doing a qualitative content analysis, which was the method that we derived and used for data analysis purposes.

Nieuwenhuis (2007, p. 101) defines content analysis as "a process of looking at data from different angles with a view to identifying keys in the text that will help us to understand and interpret the raw data". Content analysis was used in the study through an inductive process that involved coding trends and developing patterns, themes and categorisations (Patton, 2002) in the data. The themes that emerged are revealed in the next section of the chapter and constitute the findings that addressed the research questions in this chapter.

Even though the study does not fall into the category of sensitive research, we still had to ensure that basic ethical principles of research were observed especially in the area of data generation. Firstly, ethical clearance to conduct the study was sought and obtained from the management of the university who granted us the right to interview the students during normal school hours and within the premises of the university. Secondly, all participants filled in consent forms in which their rights to participate in the research were disclosed. These rights include voluntary participation in the study, their right to withdraw their participation at any stage of the study without prejudice, that their true identities will not be disclosed in the write-up, and an agreement to be tape recorded. In an effort to observe the anonymity of the participants as promised in the informed consent letter, the report in this study refers to them using pseudonyms.

The following pseudonyms were used to refer to the participants: Neo, Teboho, Dlamini, Thabo, Ndebele, and Puseletso. The order of the naming follows the same order in which the interviews were conducted with all six participants. All interviews were conducted in a neutral classroom venue and not in offices to mitigate the challenges linked to lecturer-student power dynamics and allow students to speak out freely. The ethical principles were in conformity with the premise that "The researcher remains obligated at all times to give a complete explanation of the total investigation, without pressure or unnecessary interference, in clear and intelligible language" (Kutchins, 1991, p. 111, cited in Strydom & Venter, 2004, p. 66). The goal was to ensure the full knowledge and cooperation of the participants, while also resolving or even relieving any possible tension, aggression resistance or insecurity of the participants (Strydom & Venter, 2004).

Results

After explaining in the previous section the methodology used in this study as well as the methods that were used to collect and analyse the data, this section is meant to present the findings that emerged from the analysis. The findings are presented below in a thematic manner that reflects the two research questions underpinning this study. In presenting the findings, we started with the themes that reflect answers to the first research question before proceeding to the second.

Research question one: what are students' views of integrating ICTs into learning in one Lesotho University?

Students' understanding of ICTs

When asked about their understandings of what ICTs are and their views on integrating them into their learning, all the participants demonstrated some knowledge of the concept. They first defined it as a general concept before explaining their understandings of the concept in relation to learning. As a general concept, they mostly defined it in terms of communications and information. For instance,

Ndebele noted that ICT is "an umbrella word for communicative and technology devices…" Similarly, Teboho submitted that ICT is: "All about the advancement towards communications, all the mechanisms, the machinery and all other things that have been captured to enable communication to be easy in all aspects of life".

Meanwhile, some of the participants see ICTs more as tools for socialisation than just communication. Dlamini, for instance, mentioned that: "I think ICT is a technological media where people can put their ideas and I think it becomes also socialism where we can meet and talk or access some certain material".

The examples of technologies the participants mentioned varied from hardware and software. The hardware technologies include computers, cell phones, televisions, radios, Cd roms, flash disks and microphones whilst for the software a range of elements were mentioned ranging from the internet, emails, Facebook, WhatsApp, Google, Google scholar, IMO and Wikis. These are the different forms of ICT that the range of students cited as their understanding of technologies implying they all have a working knowledge of what constitutes technology in general and educational technologies in particular.

Technology as an important tool for learning

Apart from understanding what ICT entails, all the participants in this study also see it as important for their learning. Neo, for example, stated that: "My understanding of ICT seems that we should engage more in technologies especially when doing school work and other personal stuff and getting additional information on things that maybe we will like to engage in".

She goes further to note that:

> If a lecturer used PowerPoint, it makes us get some information easily because using traditional method especially the chalkboard and stuff, if he erases something or the time he is writing the notes, you may not get what he is writing or see what he is writing but using PowerPoint, the picture gets clear.

The sentiments of Neo were corroborated by Teboho who denoted that:

> As a student, I use the internet as I said, and it really helps me a lot because nowadays the kind of university we are having, it does not have enough resources such as books that are contemporary for that matter because we need contemporary information in order to accomplish our studies. So its internet that provided us with that information.

From the view of Teboho captured above, ICTs are important in learning especially in the context of their university that is very limited in hard copy resources for learning.

Research question two: How do students in one Lesotho University integrate ICTs into learning?

Social media as an important tool for learning

Another finding was the realisation that students relied greatly on social media as an ICT tool for their learning. All the participants mentioned one form of social media or another as very important learning tools. The following forms of social media were highlighted by the participants: WhatsApp, Facebook, Imo, and Wikis. Of all these aspects of social media, WhatsApp and Facebook seem to be the most used as per the responses from the participants. Teboho, for instance, provided a very detailed account of how these two aspects of social media are used in learning:

> I just want to talk about Facebook and WhatsApp because the two seems to be the most influential ones in our university. WhatsApp, you find out that there are different groups according to classes, for instance, you will see there will be … WhatsApp group where there will be a discussion on certain matters. We are able to share materials such as PDFs we are able to post them there, videos etc. and everybody has access if he or she is part of the WhatsApp group and also Facebook. There are those groups on Facebook that we use… For instance, I am aware that I am not alone, most of the students also use Facebook as the site to get information. Like I have mentioned since I am a

development student in English language and linguistics, I need to get current information every now and then so most each and every day I go through news and Facebook to get updates.

Dlamini, on the other hand, sees WhatsApp as very convenient: "If I don't understand something, I don't have to walk to my neighbours' house or where my friends are staying; I just communicate what I do not understand and get assistance". Furthermore, Ndebele posited that "We have WhatsApp groups with which we communicate with our classmates. Maybe I want the explanation of a concept, I ask in the group and somebody responds". The implication is that students have clustered themselves around social media learning groups and use the social media for the purpose of learning. However, in spite of this benefit, some students were also of the view that the social media could be counter-productive. Puseletso, for instance, articulated this view:

> I think there are some disadvantages [of social media] because sometimes you find that we do not use them for educational purposes like on WhatsApp groups or Facebook groups someone will send something outside what the purpose of the group is like pornography and things like that on the group.

This view was supported by Thabo who stated that:

> Sometimes you will find that you will be using WhatsApp for useless things, not to school work. In case we will be having an assignment, you will concentrate on WhatsApp on useless things with your friends. Sometimes you will find out that you will not be reading, you will be entertaining yourself with Facebook.

Notwithstanding this negative side of social media, all the participants were of the opinion that the positive side of social media outweighs the negativity and therefore social media remains a very important component of their learning experience.

Presence of university-based interactive E-learning site

It was also gleaned from the data that students acknowledge university efforts in promoting ICT-based learning. This they claim is done through a university online interactive platform that they called 'thuto' [education]. Teboho defines 'thuto' as

> Learning software... a special website assigned for students and lecturers as well as the university in general to communicate. Every student has his or her own workspace, and the lecturers and everyone who is part of the University [academic community]. So, there is that communication, notices are being posted in there, assignments, syllabus and all the stuff is there.

There is a feeling among the respondents that this interactive online website is very effective for their learning. They disclosed that every registered student is provided with a 'thuto' account and amongst the things that 'thuto' provides for them are: ability to source materials put up by lecturers and even chat with lecturers via your workspace (Dlamini), receive important announcements from the SRC – student representative council, or from the faculties (Thabo), receive announcements on major events about the University (Ndebele), a drop box where students can leave a message for the lecturer as well as comments (Neo).

Another reason advanced as to why students appreciate the 'thuto' (Education) initiative is the fact that they are inducted into using the service from the beginning of their studies at the University. This induction provides them with the necessary technical skills to use the service effectively for the purpose for which it was designed. All the participants acknowledged having received such training whilst they were doing the first year. However, Ndebele was of the view that "students who reside off campus have challenges with using thuto". His explanation was however due to access to internet hot spots on campus (accessibility) rather than the competence to use the service.

Internet challenges and shortage of common computers

Considering that most of the ICT used by the students requires an internet connection, the students highlighted this as a major factor impeding the smooth integration of technologies in their learning. They disclosed that the university campus including the on-campus residences is not fully covered by internet access making it difficult for a student who cannot afford internet data to access materials from the internet or even from thuto at their will. Teboho, for example, put the number of internet hotspots areas on campus to about four, but as Dlamini complained that "The WIFI [wireless internet] sometimes you find there are very weak and have to take about five minutes to connect". This view was supported by Puseletso who suggested that "It is difficult because it's in some places not all over the university so it's difficult to access it. Sometimes we gather there by the WIFI point in large numbers and it is very slow at times".

While students mentioned that the university has a computer lab that is connected to the internet and available to students, they also complained that the number of computers in the lab is insufficient to accommodate the student population. Thabo, for instance, highlighted this plight by stating that, "Yes there are computer labs but they are very insufficient. They cannot accommodate us". The shortage of computers in the campus lab is exacerbated by the fact the lab only opens during official university hours when students are attending lectures. They bemoaned the fact that the lab is not opened after lecture hours which would have given them an opportunity to use the facility after classes. The above concern was captured by Teboho who claimed that:

> … During the day, most of the students are very busy with their school work, attending classes and all that. It is so unfair that at 16:30, the labs do close. It is so unfair because after 16:00, most students are now free and want to start studying. Some at 18:00 and 20:00. So, it will be very much important if it will open to maybe midnight.

The findings from this study have indicated that students at this university have a good working knowledge and understanding of

ICT. These understandings are linked to their use of both software and hardware forms of technologies. It is also understood that students to a great extent are keen on integrating ICTs in their learning. Most significantly, it was observed that they make use of their cell phones and personal computers through which they can access the few internet hotspots on campus for purposes of learning. With these technology gadgets, they then link each other in learning groups on social media such as WhatsApp and Facebook to either access material from the internet or simply share ideas on class work.

Discussion

It was evident that the students understood their integration of ICTs into learning from a formal and informal perspective. Thus, the students' learning through ICTs was influenced by the said two-pronged processes (Valentin, et al., 2013; Thang et al., 2016). From a formal perspective, the students used ICTs mainly for academic and educational purposes through formal platforms established by the University. 'Thuto' which literally means education is a name given to that platform. As a university regulated platform, all students were trained to use it during their first year of entry in the university. As a result, the students were also exposed to the rules which mediated relationship among members of the community (Isssroff & Scanlon, 2002).

They accessed learning materials from this platform. Students realised the benefits of using ICTs particularly the internet for making it easier for them to access information amid a lack of reading materials in their university. The internet, therefore, served as an object for the achievement of desired outcomes of learning. However, the challenges of computers' shortage and limited internet capacity negatively affected students' access to the internet. Wallet (2015) also found that the use of ICTs in Sub-Saharan Africa is compounded with multiple challenges.

Furthermore, the students viewed various social media platforms especially Facebook and WhatsApp as essential tools which facilitated learning among students. In these platforms, students shared information without assistance from their lecturers. As argued by Amry (2014) access to information anytime, anywhere in diverse formats through the use of technologies enables students to construct knowledge without assistance from an expert. This study found that Facebook and WhatsApp served as ICTs' artefacts which students used to create communities of learning. Interpreted from an activity theory perspective, the community consisted of students who reportedly used social networks to create group forums. In a collaborative relationship of knowledge construction, the students engage in a horizontal division of labour. As observed by Hardman (2005) in a horizontal division of labour students actively engage and take charge of their own learning. They share knowledge and skills as equals. However, there is also a vertical dimension in which more knowledgeable students or brighter students assisted their peers. Students played a central role in learning through autonomous as opposed to controlled and directed learning by lecturers.

It appeared that the informal learning platforms (Facebook and WhatsApp) were not entirely used for the purposes of learning and thus positioned students in a space where they could either learn or their attention was diverted to issues irrelevant to education. At times, some students posted pornography materials on social media. In line with the findings in the current study, Thang et al. (2016) also found that students sometimes use ICTs more often for social than educational purposes. At this point, it is necessary to highlight the nature of the community in this informal learning setup. The community mainly consisted of peers. Here, the rules of engagement seemed to have been unconventional. It seems that there was no line of demarcation between academic and social conversations. According to Isssroff & Scanlon (2002), the manner in which the community interact and engage in the pursuit of a given object is mediated by the rules. In the absence of such rules, the relations of knowledge construction among students could hardly be regulated.

It is additionally significant to note contradictions that came to the fore as students used ICTs in their learning. Kuutti (2001, p. 34) notes that: Contradictions manifest themselves as problems, ruptures, breakdowns, clashes. Activity theory sees contradictions as sources of development; activities are virtually always in the process of working through contradictions.

Shortage of mediating tools like computers in the university can be viewed as a contradiction between students' perspective of having well-equipped computer laboratories and the university's capability to make provision for such resources. In this sense, a contradiction arises out of the intended use of computer laboratories and students' access to these laboratories. From a subject and community relations perspective which is mediated by the rules, there were contradictions pertaining to how operating hours seemed to privilege the computer lab technicians but marginalised the students whereas the computers were intended to benefit the students. Closely related to the problem of shortage of computers was the existence of limited university internet capacity (Lesotho Government, 2013) which the students access through the wireless setup. This limitation sometimes caused inconvenience and breakdowns in students' learning. As Bodker (2001, p. 150) puts it: Breakdowns related to the use of process occur when work is interrupted by something, perhaps the tool behaves differently than was anticipated, thus causing the triggering of inappropriate operations or not triggering any at all.

When the functioning of the learning tool was interrupted, learning was also affected negatively. Students required the internet for accessing information, communication and other learning activities. It is equally noteworthy to indicate the contradictions which unfolded as a result of a two-pronged intention of using social networks among students. On the one hand, students used these networks for socialising with their peers. On the other hand, the said networks were used for academic purposes. Sometimes, students ended up socialising while the initial plan was to use social networks for learning or academic purposes. In this way, contradictions emerged.

According to Bodker (2001), contradictions in the activity serves as a driving force for learning and change. In other words, students as subjects had the potential to observe contradictions in using social media networks and therefore draw some lessons which may lead to the transformation of how they used social media. Such possible learning and change were not noted in this study even though students were aware that sometimes social use of Facebook and

WhatsApp undermined the purpose of learning. Thus, contradictions may not necessarily translate into learning and transformation.

Conclusion

This chapter concludes that students understood their integration of ICTs into learning as both a formal and informal process. Formal channels of learning through ICT platforms were those initiated and controlled by the university while students themselves initiated and regulated informal platforms. It was apparent that the students relied heavily on informal ICT tools since formal learning platforms seemed to be compounded by breakdowns and contradictions.

While the informal arrangements among students in using WhatsApp and Facebook platforms were of academic and educational benefit, the challenges relating to distractions of such noble endeavours and initiatives cannot be ignored. It is, therefore, suggested that students should have WhatsApp and Facebook forums or groups specifically dedicated to educational conversations. There is also a need for students to decide on the rules that will guide them in using WhatsApp and Facebook as a platform for learning. Such will serve as a point of reference in mediating their relationship in the use of self-regulated ICTs.

Recommendations

The findings have practical implications for the integration of ICTs into learning by students pointing to the need for the university to improve ICTs infrastructure as a way of creating an enabling environment for students. While it was evident that students had, to some level or degree, started using social media for learning, it is suggested that such an initiative would be more effective if lecturers also integrate social media into teaching. It is recommended that students, academics and university management or their representatives should work together to formulate a policy that will be used for regulation of operating computer laboratories and other ICTs' resources.

This chapter was based on the views of selected students in one university. The findings, therefore, cannot be generalised to all Lesotho universities. Thus, there is a need for further research which will provide a bigger picture of the state of ICTs integration into learning in Lesotho universities. Since this chapter only used a qualitative approach, it is recommended that future studies use a mixed methods approach.

References

Adams, L. (2003). Information and Communication Technologies in Higher Education in Africa: Initiatives and Challenges. *Journal of Higher Education in Africa*, 1(1), 195–221.

Amry, A.B. (2014). The impact of WhatsApp mobile social learning on the achievement and attitudes of female students compared with face to face learning in the classroom. *European Scientific Journal*, 10(22), 116-136.

Bellamy, R.K.E. (2001). Designing Educational Technology: Computer-mediated change. In B. A. Nardi (ed.), *Context and Consciousness: Activity theory and human-computer interaction* (pp.123-146). Cambridge: The MIT Press.

Bodker, S. (2001). Applying activity theory to video analysis: how to make sense of video data in HCI. In B. A. Nardi (ed.), *Context and Consciousness: Activity theory and human-computer interaction* (pp.147-174). Cambridge: The MIT Press.

Cohen, L., Manion, L., & Morrison, K. (2007). *Research methods in education* (6th ed). New York: Routledge.

Cohen, L., Manion, L., & Morrison, K. (2011). *Research methods in education* (7th ed). New York: Routledge.

Creswell, J. W. (2014). *Research design qualitative, quantitative, and mixed methods approaches* (4th ed). Thousand Oaks CA: Sage Publications.

Dabbagh, N., & Kitsantas, A. (2012). Personal Learning Environments, social media, and self-regulated learning: A natural formula for connecting formal and informal learning. *The Internet and higher education*, 15(1), 3-8.

Denzin, N., & Lincoln, Y. (2005). Introduction: the discipline and practice of qualitative research. In N. Denzin & Y. Lincoln (eds), *Strategies of qualitative inquiry* (3rd ed., pp. 1-44). London: Sage Publication.

De Vos, A.S., Strydom, H., Fouché, C.B., & Delport, C.S.L. (2005). *Research at grass roots: for the social sciences and human service professions.* Cape Town: Van Shaik Publisher.

Gikas, J., & Grant, M.M. (2013). Mobile computing devices in higher education: Student perspectives on learning with cell phones, smartphones & social media. *Internet and Higher Education*, 19, 18-26.

Hardman, J. (2005). Activity theory as a potential framework for technology research in an unequal terrain. *South African Journal of Higher Education*, 19(2), 378-392.

Hashim, H., & Jones, H. L. (2007). Activity theory: a framework for qualitative analysis. *4th International qualitative research convention.* Malaysia: Hilton.

Henning, E. (2004). *Finding your way in qualitative research* (First ed). Cape Town: Van Shaik Publishers.

Isssroff, K., & Scanlon, E. (2002). Using technology in higher education: An activity theory perspective. *Journal of Computer Assisted Learning*, 18, 77-83.

Joo, Y. J., Kim, N., & Kim, N. H. (2016). Factors predicting online university students' use of a mobile learning management system (m-LMS). *Educational Technology Research and Development*, 64, 611-630.

Kuuti, K. (2001). Activity Theory as a potential framework for human-computer interaction research. In B. A. Nardi, *Context and consciousness: activity theory and human-computer interaction* (pp.17-44). Cambridge: The MIT Press.

Lesotho Ministry of Communications, Science and Technology. (2005). *Lesotho ICT Policy.* Ministry of Communications and Information, Lesotho Printing works. Retrieved 26 September 2016 from www.lesotho.gov.ls

Lesotho Government, (2013). Higher Education Policy for the Kingdom of Lesotho. Retrieved 26 September, from http://www.che.ac.ls/documents/CHE%20Policy%20(2013).pdf

Maoba, M. L. (2009). *Lecturers' experiences of integrating information and communication technology (ICT) into teaching at a college of education.* Masters. Dissertation, University of KwaZulu-Natal, Durban.

Maposa, C., & Mudzielwana, N. P. (2014). Professionalisation of Teaching in Universities: a compelling case. *International Educational Sciences*, 6(1), 65-73.

McMillan, J. (2009). Through an activity theory lens: conceptualizing service learning as 'boundary work. *International Journal of Community Research and Engagement, 1*(2), 39–60.

Nieuwenhuis, J. (2007). Qualitative research designs and data gathering techniques, in K. Maree (ed), *First steps in research* (70-92). Pretoria: Van Shaik Publishers.

Patton, M.Q. (2002). *Qualitative research and evaluation methods.* Thousand Oaks: Sage.

Strydom, H., & Venter, L. (2004). Ethical aspects of research in the social sciences and human service professions. In A.S. De Vos (ed), *research at grass roots: for the social sciences and human service professions* (pp.62-75). Van Shaik Publishers: Cape Town.

Taleba, Z., & Sohrabib, A. (2012). Learning on the move: the use of mobile technology to support learning for university students. *Procedia - Social and Behavioral Sciences*, 69, 1102-1109.

Thang, S. M., Lee, K.W., Murugaiah, P., Jaafar, N.M., Tan, C.K., & Bukhari, N.I.A. (2016). ICT Tools Patterns of Use among Malaysian ESL Undergraduates. *Journal of Language Studies*, 16(1), 49-65.

Vajargah, K.F., Jahani, S., & Azadmanesh, N. (2010). Application of ICTs in teaching and learning at University level: the case of Shahid Beheshti University. *The Turkish Online Journal of Educational Technology*, 9(3), 33-39.

Valentín, A., Mateos, P.M., González-Tablas, M.M., Pérez, L., López, E., & García, I., (2013). Motivation and learning strategies in the use of ICTs among university students. *Computers & Education, 61*, 52-58.

Wallet, P. (2015). *Information and Communication Technology (ICT) in education in sub-Saharan Africa: a comparative analysis of basic e-readiness in schools*. UNESCO Institute for Statistics. Retrieved 20 November 2016 from http://dx.doi.org/10.15220/978-92-9189-178-8-en.

Chapter 3

Prior access to modern learning technologies as a predictor of Post-Admission Cognitive Dissonance in African universities: Evidence from Namibia and Zimbabwe

Fanny Saruchera
&
Africa Makasi

Abstract

This paper investigates the effect of prior access to modern learning technologies as a predictor of post-admission cognitive dissonance (PACD) and the subsequent implications on students' performance at tertiary institutions. Self-administered questionnaires were distributed to 384 first year students systematically selected using a two-stage sampling technique from two technology universities in Namibia and Zimbabwe. A filter question was used to separate students who had prior access to any form of modern learning technology (in this case computer appreciation and online learning technologies). Accordingly, a total of 200 students confirmed their total lack of prior access to any modern learning technologies before enrolling at university. Students who had prior access to computers and other learning gadgets during their high school education formed one group of 184 students (control group) while the other made up of students who had no prior exposure to computers made the experimental group. The groups were deliberately equally split in order validate the results of the study. Findings from the research revealed that over 80% of students who had no access to technology displayed high levels of post enrolment dissonance. This was in sharp contrast to the results obtained from the control group (made up of students with prior access to computers) who displayed a high degree of confidence and daring to learn. The research further revealed that over 89% of students who lacked prior access to technology were performing below average while some did not bother even to do their assigned work primarily due to lack of technical knowledge. Based on these findings, the study proposes a number of recommendations to African higher learning institutions to nip post-admission dissonance in the bud while making efforts to implement consonant-building strategies. This paper adds to existing knowledge on the theory of cognitive dissonance and its relevance in educational business sense in general and educational marketing practice in particular. The unpleasant feelings created by rival thoughts often lead students to deregister and in some fatal cases result in students committing suicide as a result of failure to manage the impact of the mental tension. This negative experience, the study reveals, has been fuelled by lack of prior access to modern learning technologies such as computers and lap tops which students are almost entirely compelled to use upon enrolment at universities.

Keywords: dissonance, learning technologies, post-admission dissonance, university.

Introduction and Background

The choice of an institution for higher education, as is the selection of a particular degree programme to pursue within that institution, is a decision of considerable importance for most individuals (Conklin, 2014). According to Mitchell (2003) the presence of this phenomenon and subsequent strategies to manage it is vital to student retention efforts. Cognitive dissonance theory suggests that consumers experience tension following a difficult decision and may behave in some strange ways in an effort to reduce the dissonance (Fill, 2002). The thrust of cognitive dissonance theory is that dissonance is likely to occur after a choice has been made. With modern technologies now dictating the pace and magnitude of commerce, the effect of the phenomenon has been further exacerbated. Its presence at universities and other institutions of higher learning requires urgent enquiry which fosters a conducive learning environment to all irrespective of background (Conklin,

2014). A review of extant literature reveals that dissonance can occur in the pre-purchase, purchase, and post-purchase phases. Thus in the context of admission, dissonance could occur in the pre-admission, admission and post-admission phases. The present study seeks to explore the effect of prior access to modern learning technologies as a predictor of post-admission cognitive dissonance (PACD) with evidence provided by first year students at two conveniently selected African Universities.

Research Background

With the increasing population of universities in Africa and worldwide pitted against an increasing number of potential students, the choice of a university to study for a particular degree programme is proving quite a daunting task (Maringe & Carter, 2007; Owusu, 2012). However, the increase in the number of universities has not been proportionate - many students continue to be churned out from thousands of high schools across the continent all subsequently converging to queue and compete for the few places offered by a few universities. However, despite offering similar curricula, these high schools are structured in different ways with some providing advanced learning methods aided by cutting edge technology while others are still offering studies in the most rudimentary way.

Notwithstanding this anomaly and despite the challenges of resources faced by some students during their high school learning period, most of them excel in their studies and soon find their way to universities. The emerging picture paints a cautionary tale, particularly in regard to the reality of digital equity and social justice in the developing world context (Conklin, 2014). On the surface, it appears their lack of prior access to modern learning technologies is never seen as a hindrance towards enrolment at universities until the first few days after enrolment when the use of learning technologies is made the norm at almost all universities in Namibia and Zimbabwe if not the entire sub-region. Signs of post-enrolment dissonance will then start to show.

Given this background the main objective of this study is to establish the effect of prior access to modern learning technologies as a predictor of post enrolment dissonance in African Universities with Namibia and Zimbabwe being used as cases studies. This calls for establishing the gaps that exists between students' expectations against institutional strategies so as to recommend strategies to close such gaps. The study commences with a brief review of the theory forming the framework of the concept of cognitive dissonance, which serves as a basis for developing empirical evidence. This is then followed by an explanation of the research methodology adopted, then discussion of the main findings. The study winds up with the main conclusions and recommendations.

Theoretical Framework

Theory of Cognitive Dissonance

The theory of cognitive dissonance back-dates to the late 40's and a great deal of inauguration credit has been attributed to Festinger (1957). Much research interest in the subject dominated the social psychology scenes from the 1950s and intensified in the 70's (Anderson, 1973; Fishbein & Ajzen, 1976; Fishbein, 1977; Houston & Rothschild, 1978). The theory indeed has been a recurring theme in psychology and consumer marketing literature (O'Neill & Palmer, 2004) as it has drawn attention from scientists, psychologists and marketers over the last half century. According to Gbadamosi (2009), the cognitive dissonance theory has been profoundly explored in a multitude of academic areas such as psychology (Balcetis & Dunning, 2007; Harmon-Jones & Harmon-Jones, 2008) and marketing (Lindsey-Mullikin, 2003; O'Neill & Palmer, 2004). Thus despite it being an 'old, new' concept, the theory appears more relevant today than ever as consumerism and consumer education are on the rise hence the researchers' renewed interest in the theory, but now focusing on educational technology access.

Cognitive Dissonance and its Underpinning Theories Explored

The original statement of the cognitive dissonance theory (Festinger, 1957) proposed that dissonant relations between cognitions have the potential to create a negative effect that motivates individuals to make attempts to reduce the discrepancies between cognitions. Festinger (1957) clearly defined cognitive dissonance as a psychological state, which refers to the discomfort felt at a discrepancy between what individuals already know or believe, and new information. He suggested that cognitions are dissonant with one another when they "do not fit together", or when they are inconsistent with each other or contradict one another. In simpler terms, Festinger (1957) put forward that, when an individual holds two or more elements of knowledge that are relevant to each other but inconsistent with one another, a state of discomfort is created, thus dissonance.

This situation makes the individuals experience an unpleasant state of tension. However, Dechawatanapaisal and Siengthai (2006) predict that people generally prefer consonance so they will seek a stable state where there is a minimum dissonance to make such inconsistent cognitions fit together. Concisely, Festinger's theory can be conceptualized in two distinguishable ways: dissonance as psychological discomfort and dissonance as arousal (Elliot & Devine, 1994). O'Neill and Palmer (2004) have exposed the raging debate between scientists' and consumer marketer's views and perspectives on the cognitive dissonance theory. While scientists have questioned the precise nature of the dissonance theory and its explanations (Wilkie, 2000), marketers argue that cognitive dissonance exists and it has to be managed. In fact, economic psychologists believe that informed and knowledgeable consumers are expected to experience less cognitive dissonance after purchase of a product or service (Selnes & Troye, 1989).

However, Shultz and Lepper (1992, 1996) as cited in Shultz, Léveillé and Lepper (1999) presented a computational, constraint satisfaction model of these and other cognitive dissonance phenomena. In addition to replicating the results of previous studies, simulations generated by this consonance model suggest a number of new and more precise predictions about the consequences of decisions. Accordingly, these simulations predict differences in the specific form of dissonance reduction as a function of the general level of attractiveness of the choice options. Whether a person is choosing, between two competing options, such predictions not only constitute a highly rigorous test of the consonance model but also illustrate how this model can be useful for guiding contemporary psychological research.

Much later, Harmon-Jones and Harmon-Jones (2008) traced the development of the theory from self-consistency, self-affirmation, and aversion consequences revisions – challenged each revision and reviewed the action-based model, which is basically in support of the Festinger's (1957) original contributions. Most of these models have had a general focus and a few studies (Kotler, 1979; Lawley & Blight, 1997) have developed models that are specific to cognitive dissonance in tertiary institutions, worst still in developing economies where prior exposure to technologies often used at Universities are potential contributory factors towards dissonance or lack of it. Lawley and Blight (1997) developed the model of university selection by international students. The emphasis of these and other related models (Hill & O'Sullivan, 1999) was however on the pre-purchase phase of the consumer decision-making process. In contrast, the focus of the present study is the post-purchase phase of the consumer decision-making process with guidance from the existing models suggested by many of the pioneer authors. For instance the factors and variables suggested in the conceptual model have been translated to become key determinants in post-admission behaviour by tertiary institution students against the background of prior exposure to learning technologies.

Digital access and post admission dissonance

The ongoing global impetus towards increased digital access and the incremental uptake of ICTs into the traditional higher education space is not only reshaping our understanding of education globally, but it is also evidencing, through research and the benefits of time, a more sober and realistic portrayal of the affordances of digital access and technology in higher education (Conklin, 2014). The emerging picture paints a cautionary tale, particularly in regard to the lived reality of digital equity and social justice in the developing world context (Conklin, 2014). Digital access and the ability to embrace technologies are thus a predictor of post admission dissonance and potentially the future flourishing of Africa. The impact of the digital revolution on higher education has contributed to its internationalization and commodification to the extent that is has become a multinational export industry, meriting its own category in the General Agreement on Trade and Services (GATS) (Altbach, 2001).

However, despite the promise of technology to break the "Iron Triangle" of "Access, Cost and Quality" (Alves & Raposo, 2009), it is becoming increasingly evident that the divide between the so-called "developed "and "developing "nations, has in fact deepened, largely as a result of a continuing lack of access to the internet in the developing world. In Africa, this challenge is driven by the wide divide between the rich and the poor with some students coming from very poor backgrounds lacking exposure to basic learning technologies. This in turn affects their post enrolment evaluation which leads them to cognitive dissonance. There is a yawning gulf globally and nationally, between those who have access to the internet and those who do not and even where there is access, between its speed, reliability, cost and affordability (Alves & Raposo, 2009). Even within countries such as South Africa, where 52% of people purportedly have access to the internet at home, this is likely to be via mobile phones connecting to cellular providers' masts and not via personal computers or other such devices connecting via Wi-Fi (Botha, 2016). Most homes in Southern Africa do not have Wi-Fi. Furthermore, connection and download speed remain hugely problematic. This is especially challenging in regard to establishing an efficient and an effective transactional environment for students, not to mention a quality teaching and learning (and assessment) environment.

Factors Affecting Choice of Tertiary Institutions

According to the University selection model, Kotler (1979) propounds that a potential student first seeks and receives information obtains an initial awareness of the university, which then translates into expanded university awareness as the prospective student gets specific college information. This then leads to university choice as the student gets admitted into the university system. According to Kotler (1979), once the university is chosen, the process ends. The subsequent models (Lawley, 1997; Lawley & Blight, 1997) support the views of Kotler (1979), even though they edify the factors influencing the process of selecting a university to include variables such as academic factors and programme variety.

The researchers entirely agree with Singh (2003) along with Wilkins and Balakrishnan (2013) who noted that student satisfaction or dissatisfaction is not determined solely by the students' teaching and learning experiences but rather by their overall experiences as a customer of a particular institution. In a study conducted in Poland, Sojkin, Bartkowiak, and Skuza (2012) identified social conditions and educational facilities among the key determinants of student satisfaction in higher education. Preceding studies in the USA found that student perceptions of institutional ability to provide a good intellectual environment positively affect their level of satisfaction (Hartman & Schmidt, 1995). Wells and Daunt (2011) propose a conceptual model where the physical environment of a higher educational institution (which incorporates layout and design factors and general ambient factors) can lead to student satisfaction as an outcome.

They found that a sample of UK students was concerned with comfort and equipment in their learning environments. These and other related factors have also been proven by studies pertaining developing economies such as Ghana (Owusu, 2012). Thus the quality of any "moments of truth" (Parasuraman, Zeithaml & Berry, 1988) experienced by customers form part of their overall impression of the whole service provided and this impact evaluation of the service during and post-purchase i.e. post-admission in case of tertiary institutions' service delivery. Based on the extant literature, it evident that the role of prior access to modern learning technologies, which eventually becomes a dominant feature in teaching and learning at universities, remains unexplored.

Factors Influencing Choice of Programme of Study

Over and above factors affecting their choice of tertiary institutions, tertiary institution applicants consider many factors before they finally settle on a particular programme of study (Owusu, 2012), even though their entry qualifications' subject combination normally determines the choice of programmes that they could pursue at tertiary institutions. Some applicants have more programmes to choose from than others as a result of their subject combination. Thus applicants with a wider choice would normally have a high probability of suffering post-admission dissonance due to the feeling that they could have opted for better programmes and / or institutions.

Other factors include the student's interest in the programmes that they could pursue a particular career in life (Saunders, Hamilton & Lancaster, 1978; Karren, 2007; Owusu, 2012). Others also choose particular programmes because they believe that they are likely to get a job if they pursue such programmes (Jon, 2006). Besides the above factors, some applicants decide to pursue certain programmes as a result of the expectation of their parents (Jon, 2006; Schweitzer, Griffin, Ancis & Thomas, 1999). Despite an appreciation of these and other factors, Brennan, (2001) maintains that little research has been undertaken to evaluate students' capacity to undertake decision-making about their courses and institutions in an informed and empowered manner, which current researchers believe have contributed to a great deal of cognitive dissonance amongst students.

Cognitive Dissonance in Tertiary Institutions' Admission

Post-purchase behaviour of customers is associated with the evaluation of the choice made by the customer (Conklin, 2014). Consumers tend to re-think their decisions in light of the experience with the product and service during this stage due to uncertainty of the wisdom of their decisions, thus satisfaction becomes crucial in this post-purchase assessment. For students in transition to university, cognitive dissonance might be generated if the students' expectations of the institution as well as programme expectations are not fulfilled (Conklin, 2014). Consequently, the understanding of students' expertise, and therefore their ability to undertake the highly complex decision-making task of choosing a university, is important to marketers and university administrators alike. The researchers agree with Brennan (2001) that research into student decision-making is indeed still in its infancy in most countries, especially in developing countries, which is the focus of this research. Alba and Hutchinson (1987) suggest that there are two types of consumer knowledge: familiarity, which is based on experience with the product or product class; and expertise, which is based on the ability to perform product-related tasks.

Expertise is comprised of subjective knowledge; that is, the consumer may believe they have knowledge of the product class (Mitchell & Dacin, 1996). In addition, expertise comprises objective knowledge; that is, when the consumer has product-related memories which are accurate and according to Rao and Sieben (1992), these can be measured by some objective means. Knowledge of both types (including computer knowledge) leads to expertise in a product-related task. It is indeed necessary to consider both objective and subjective knowledge due to the likelihood of inaccuracy in determining levels of subjective knowledge (Selnes & Troye, 1989). However, in the consumer research domain it is relatively straightforward to determine a relationship between subject related experiences and the development of objective expertise. Consumer confusion would however result in cases where the consumers become overwhelmed with information and this would increase the chances of consumers making sub-optimum decisions, a dilemma which Drummond (2004) argues it confronts the higher education sector worldwide.

In order to reduce the dissonance, Festinger (1957) suggests three modes and these include seeking constant information, attitude change and trivializing (Lindsey-Mullikin, 2003). Frijda, Manstead and Bem (2000) posit that dissonance reduction involves subtracting dissonant cognitions, adding consonant cognitions, and decreasing the importance of dissonant cognitions. A review by Wilkins and Balakrishnan (2013) found that tertiary institutions that achieve student satisfaction can benefit in a number of ways, for example, satisfied students are less likely to drop out (Tinto, 1993) after admission; more likely to achieve higher grades (Bean & Bradley, 1986); engage in positive word-of-mouth and collaborate with the institution after they graduate (Alves & Raposo, 2009). The increase in use of social networking and consumer web sites such as RateMyProfessors.com has greatly promoted electronic word-of-mouth (Wilkins & Epps, 2011). Students experiencing cognitive dissonance may use a number of strategies to attempt to reduce it. They may seek out reassurance and opinions from others to confirm the wisdom of their purchase decision, lower their attitudes or opinions of the un-chosen alternative, deny or distort any information that does not support the choice they made, or look for information that does support their choice. However, post admission dissonance is quite difficult to manage than to detect.

Conceptual framework

With guidance from the literature reviewed above, Figure 1 shows the researchers' conceptual framework of this research.

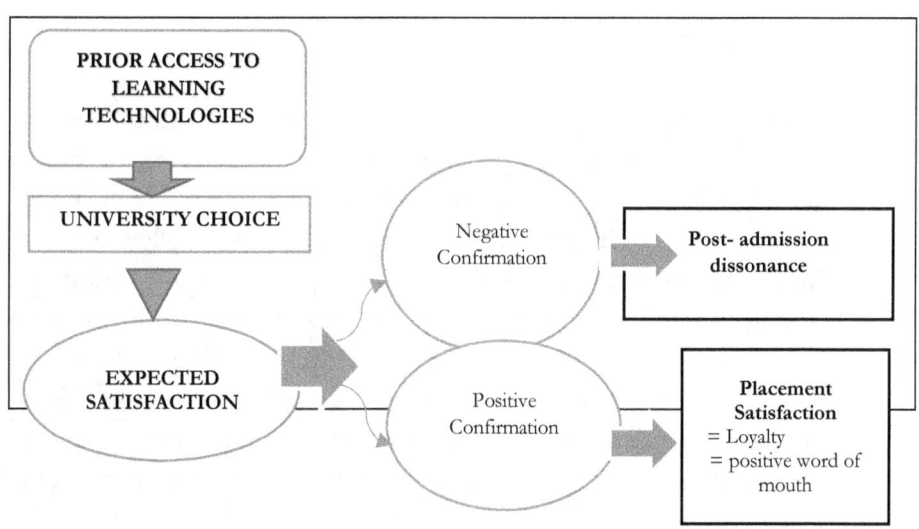

Figure 1: Conceptual Framework
Source: *Developed for the purposes of the study*

The conceptual model on Figure 1 suggests that prior access to modern learning technologies has a direct effect on post admission dissonance. Dissonance is a function of the conflicting mental thoughts and emotions. Festinger (1957) clearly defined cognitive dissonance as a psychological state, which refers to the discomfort felt at a discrepancy between what individuals already know or believe, and new information. He suggested that cognitions are dissonant with one another when they "do not fit together", or when they are inconsistent with each other or contradict one another. The thrust of cognitive dissonance theory is that dissonance is likely to occur after a choice has been made, and will reflect a natural occurrence because the choice has been made (Gilbert, 2003). A positive confirmation of the already existing conflicting thoughts will trigger post-purchase dissonance while a negative confirmation results in satisfaction through loyalty and the satisfied customer (student) will spread positive word of mouth regarding the institution. Marketing's role is to reduce post-purchase dissonance through cognitive consonant building strategies such as endorsements by successful former students of their universities.

Methodology

The main objective of the study was to assess the effect of prior access to modern learning technologies as a predictor of post-admission dissonance of students at two universities in Namibia and Zimbabwe. Accordingly; the study hypothesised the following: H_1: There is a positive relationship between prior access to modern learning technologies and the degree of post-enrolment dissonance by students at Universities. The main research question is: "What is the effect of prior access to modern learning technologies on student post-admission dissonance at universities?" In addition to this main research question, the research also established how dissonance can be managed going forward.

Self-administered questionnaires were distributed to 384 first year students systematically selected using a two stage sampling technique from two technology universities in Namibia and Zimbabwe, where the researchers are currently placed. A filter question was used to separate students who had prior access to any form of modern learning technology (in this case computer appreciation and online learning technologies). Accordingly a total of 200 students confirmed their total lack of prior access to any modern learning technologies before enrolling at University. Students who had prior access to computers and other learning gadgets during their high school education formed one group of 184 students (control group) while the other made up of students who had no prior exposure to computers made the experimental group. The groups were split in order validate the results of the study. The sample size was determined using recommendations from Krejcie and Morgan (1970) model for sample size determination. The choice of first year students was deliberate as post purchase dissonance tends to be high upon enrolling than when one has already gone three or four years into his or her studies. Fully structured questionnaires were personally administered to the students in lecture halls, through the assistance of trained research assistants. Students were encouraged to attempt all questions. The completed questionnaires were then collected after all students had finished completing them. This helped in recording a 100% response rate. A two –stage sampling technique was used. First, using a specially designed filtering question, only those students who had indicated that they did not consider the university as their first choice were analysed. The second stage involved randomly selecting students to assess their attitude towards learning and their respective performances.

The research approach was quantitative and the research design took a survey perspective. The choice of the approach and design were motivated by the research question under study; being the need to explore the effect of prior access to learning technologies on post admission dissonance. Prior studies (Niekerk & Blignaut, 2014; Karen, 2007) used similar methodologies and hence the justification for the use of similar approach and design in the current study. The choice of two institutions in Namibia and Zimbabwe was purely based on convenience. All collected data was entered into SPSS (version 22) for further analysis and extraction of information relating to the research objectives and hypothesis formulated.

In this study, several ethical issues were considered including the need for maintaining respondent confidentiality, obtaining prior consent from the respondents as well as protection of the respondent identities. Accordingly, biographical questions on the questionnaire did not ask respondents to identify themselves.

Results and Discussion

The reliability of the research was tested and a Cronbach's alpha value of 0.725 was recorded indicating that the questionnaire was highly reliable. While results recorded from students who had prior access to technology showed little or no negative attitude towards assignments and learning in general, results from the experimental group showed otherwise. The control group of 184 students was used to validate the results from the experimental group of 200 students. The results showed that there is a strong relationship between students' attitudes (as a result of dissonance) and their overall performance as reflected by Table 1. The t-tests reflected this strong association as all significant values was 0.001

Table 1: One Sample *t*-Test.

	Test Value = 0					
					95% Confidence Interval of the Difference	
	t	Df	Sig. (2-tailed)	Mean Difference	Lower	Upper
Attitude towards assignments	106.504	29	.000	4.933	4.84	5.03
Research's importance	87.958	29	.000	4.900	4.79	5.01
Importance of deadlines	106.504	29	.000	4.933	4.84	5.03
Course content	87.958	29	.000	4.900	4.79	5.01
Relationship with other	19.746	29	.000	1.100	.99	1.21
Actual performance in assignments	19.746	29	.000	1.100	.99	1.21
Actual performance in research	19.746	29	.000	1.100	.99	1.21
Actual performance in group work	19.746	29	.000	1.100	.99	1.21
Actual attendance	16.858	29	.000	1.167	1.03	1.31

The students admitted that their attitudes towards assignments were poor, partly because naturally, assignments demanded them to research using modern learning technologies such as computers. This was also further confirmed by the poor performance in their assignments as shown on Table 2 below. The question was: *"Do you agree that assignments help you to perform better in the final examination?"*

Table 2: Attitude towards assignments * Actual performance in assignments Cross tabulation

		Actual performance in assignments		Total
		Very Poor	Neither Good nor bad	
Attitude towards assignments	Disagree	50	0	50
	Strongly disagree	150	0	150
Total		200	0	200

In order to assess the correlation between students' attitudes, and their performances, a Pearson's correlation was done at $p=001$. Table 3 shows strong positive correlations were recorded between the students' attendance and their performance in their assignments at 0.745. Further, a strong relationship between the quality of assignments has been attributed by to the depth of researches conducted the students as reflected by a strong correlation factor of 0.630. However, the research found negative correlations between the importance of deadlines and the students' attitude towards assignments. This result ratifies the effects of prior access to learning technologies on post-enrolment dissonance as students do not see the relevance of deadlines when assignments are given.

Table 3: Correlation analysis

		Attitude towards assignments	Importance of deadlines	Actual performance in assignments	Actual performance in research	Actual attendance
Attitude towards assignments	Pearson Correlation	1	.071	.089	.089	.239
	Sig. (2-tailed)		.708	.640	.640	.203
	N	200	200	200	200	200
Importance of deadlines	Pearson Correlation	.071	1	.089	.089	.120
	Sig. (2-tailed)	.708		.640	.640	.529
	N	200	200	200	200	200
Actual performance in assignments	Pearson Correlation	.089	.089	1	.630**	.745**
	Sig. (2-tailed)	.640	.640		.000	.000
	N	200	200	200	200	200
Actual performance in research	Pearson Correlation	.890	.890	.630**	1	.447*
	Sig. (2-tailed)	.640	.640	.000		.013
	N	200	200	200	200	200
Actual attendance	Pearson Correlation	.239	.120	.745**	.447*	1
	Sig. (2-tailed)	.203	.529	.000	.013	
	N	200	200	200	200	200

** Correlation is significant at the 0.01 level (2-tailed).

* Correlation is significant at the 0.05 level (2-tailed).

Results from the correlation analysis indicated positive correlations between all the constructs being tested. For example, a strong positive correlation of 89% was shown to exist between actual performance in research and attitude towards assignments and the importance of meeting deadlines. This particular test was done at 1% level of significance. Results from Table 3 also show that the actual performance of the students in their assignments could have been contributed by their low attendance to classes as witnessed by a strong correlation of 75%; with a 99% level of confidence.

Conclusion

The study hypothesized that there is a positive relationship between prior access to modern learning technologies and the degree of post-enrolment dissonance by students at universities. Findings from the study provide positive affirmation to the hypothesis as supported by results from the simple correlation analysis conducted. Further conclusions are that prior exposure to modern leaning technologies spurs the student to do assignments and conduct research as demanded. The effect of prior access to technologies was seen as having not only a physical effect on the student but also a psychological one as students with little or no prior access to modern learning technologies showed negative attitudes towards writing their assignments. This could be exacerbated by the fact since most university assignments require students to research online, students with limited computer knowledge often find the process cumbersome and thus the development of negative attitudes.

Recommendations

The current emphasis on digital equity through access to and the uptake of ICTs in higher education may provide the solution to post admission dissonance at universities in Africa. Like any other customer, students also go through the same experience of encountering conflicting emotions upon enrolling at universities.

Based on the conclusions above, management at all universities should implement consonant-building strategies targeted at the over 60% students who have displayed high degrees of post-admission dissonance from the sampled students. Such programmes can take the form of academic support and advisory services that will provide comprehensive academic support and career guidance services to students in an effort to help them successfully attain their educational objectives. Universities may also need to take time to come up with basic computer appreciation training programmes dusting the first week of enrolment in order help those who will be coming from disadvantaged high schools. Based on the study findings, we predict that if not properly managed, post-admission cognitive dissonance would translate to post-graduation cognitive dissonance, a situation where a student, even after graduation, still feels they made a wrong decision for life.

Niekerk and Blignaut (2014) talk of integrating information and communication technology in education. Institutions must respond to the kinds of students they are dealing with now, be aware of who they are, how they think, and how they feel. Knowing more about this new generation is crucial for student recruitment and delivering the kinds of educational and social services they need. The impact of technology and social media especially in this generation Y type of students cannot be overruled. Information regarding their admission places and programmes quickly spread across social media platforms such as WhatsApp and Facebook. This either confirms or disconfirms the post-admission dissonance that the student might be experiencing. About 80% of the respondents indicated that they could be better off if they would have not known that their colleagues had been admitted at institutions to which they wished they had also been admitted. However, with social media becoming the order of the day, communication has been made easier and this only fuels their negative thoughts and experiences.

References

Alba, Joseph W., & J. Wesley Hutchinson. Dimensions of consumer expertise. (1987). *Journal of consumer research, 13*(4), 411-454.

Altbach, P. G. (2001). Higher education and the WTO: Globalization runs amok. *International Higher Education, 23*(1), 2-4.

Alves, H., & Raposo, M. (2009). The measurement of the construct satisfaction in higher education. *The Service Industries Journal,* 29(2), 203-18.

Anderson, R. E. (1973). Consumer dissatisfaction: The effect of disconfirmed expectancy on perceived product performance. *Journal of Marketing Research, 10*(1), 38-44.

Balcetis, E., & Dunning, D. (2007). Cognitive dissonance and the perception of natural environments. *Psychological Science*, *18*(10), 917-921.

Bean, J. P., & Bradley, R. K. (1986). Untangling the satisfaction-performance relationship for college students. *Journal of Higher Education*, *57*(4), 393-412.

Botha, J. (2016). Digital equity and social justice: Whose reality? Reflections from South Africa. In *33rd International Conference of Innovation, Practice and Research in the Use of Educational Technologies in Tertiary Education* (p. 76).

Brennan, L. (2001). Choosing a University Course: First year students' expertise and information search activity. *Higher Education Research & Development*, *20*(2), 217-224.

Conklin, C. L. (2014). *Promised Versus Actual College Experience: The Role of Social Media in Pre and Post-enrolment Experiences*. Rochester Institute of Technology Scholar Works

Dechawatanapaisal, D., & Siengthai, S. (2006). The impact of cognitive dissonance on learning work behaviour. *Journal of Workplace Learning*, *18*(1), 2006, 42-54.

Drummond, G. (2004). Consumer confusion: reduction strategies in higher education. *International Journal of Education Management*, *18*(5), 317-323.

Elliot, A. J., & Devine, P.G. (1994). On the motivational nature of cognitive dissonance: dissonance of psychological discomfort. *Journal of Personality and Social Psychology*, *67*(1), 382-94.

Festinger, L. (1957). *The Theory of Cognitive Dissonance*. Stanford, CA: Stanford University Press.

Fill, C. (2002). *Marketing Communications: Contexts, Strategies and Applications*. (3rd ed.). London: Prentice Hall.

Fishbein, M. (1977). *Consumer Beliefs and Behaviour with Respect to Cigarette Smoking:* A Critical Analysis of the Public Literature, Staff Report of the Federal Trade Commission, May, 1977.

Fishbein, M., & Ajzen, I. (1976). *Belief, Attitude, Intention and Behaviour: An Introduction to Theory and Research, Reading, Mass*. Boston: Addison-Wesley Publishing Co.

Frijda, N. H., Manstead, A. S., & Bem, S. (Eds.). (2000). *Emotions and beliefs: How feelings influence thoughts*. Cambridge: Cambridge University Press.

Gbadamosi, A. (2009). Cognitive dissonance: The implicit explication in low-income consumers' shopping behaviour for "low-involvement" grocery products. *International Journal of Retail & Distribution Management, 37*(12), 1077-1095.

Gilbert, D. (2003). *Retail Marketing Management*. Second Edition. London: Prentice Hall.

Harmon-Jones, E., & Harmon-Jones, C. (2007). Cognitive dissonance theory after 50 years of development. *Zeitschrift für Sozialpsychologie, 38*(1), 7-16.

Hartman, D. E., & Schmidt, S.L. (1995). Understanding student/alumni satisfaction from a consumer's perspective: the effects of institutional performance and program outcomes. *Research in Higher Education, 36*(2), 197-217.

Hill, E., & O'Sullivan, T. (1999). *Marketing*. (2nd ed.). New York: Longman.

Houston, M. J., & Rothschild, M.L. (1978). Conceptual and Methodological Perspectives on Involvement *in* S. Jain, ed. Research Frontiers in Marketing: Dialogues and Directions, 1978 Educators. *Proceedings, Chicago: American Marketing Association*, 184-187.

Jon, S. (2006). Why am I here? Students Choice in the Biosciences. *Bioscience Educational Journal, 7*(1), 4 -7.

Karen, J. (2007). Factors Influencing Students Choice(s) of Experimental Science Subjects within the International Baccalaureate Diploma Programme. *Journal of Research in International Education, 6*(1), 9-39.

Kotler, P. (1979). Strategies for introducing marketing into non-profit organizations. *The Journal of Marketing*, 37-44.

Krejcie, R. V., & Morgan, D. W. (1970). Determining sample size for research activities. *Educational and psychological measurement, 30*(3), 607-610.

Lawley, M. (1997). *Thai and Malaysian students' perceptions of overseas study destinations: an exploratory study* (Doctoral dissertation, University of Southern Queensland).

Lawley, M. A., & Blight, D. (1997). *International students: reasons for choice of an overseas study destination.* IDP Education Australia.

Lindsey-Mullikin, J. (2003). Beyond reference pricing: understanding consumers' encounters with unexpected prices. *Journal of Product & Brand Management. 12*(3), 140-53.

Maringe, F., & Carter, S. (2007). International Students motivation for studying in UK Higher Education: Insights into the choice and decision making of African students. *International Journal of Education Management, 21*(6), 459.

Mitchell, A. A., & Dacin, P. A. (1996). The assessment of alternative measures of consumer expertise. *Journal of Consumer Research, 23*(3), 219-239.

Mitchell, M. A. (2003). *Cognitive Dissonance and the University Experience.* Retrieved from http://www.swlearning.com/marketing/gitm/gitm4e05_08.html.

Niekerk, M., & Blignaut, S. (2014). A framework for Information and Communication Technology integration in schools through teacher professional development. *Africa Education Review, (11)*2, 236-253.

O'Neill, M., & Palmer, A. (2004). Cognitive dissonance and the stability of service quality perceptions. *Journal of Services Marketing, 18*(6), 433-449.

Owusu, A. (2012). Factors influencing the Choice of Tertiary Education in Ghana: A Case Study of Kumasi Polytechnic. *International Journal of Business and Management Tomorrow, 2*(4), 1-10.

Parasuraman, A., Zeithaml, V. A., & Berry, L. L. (1988). SERVQUAL: a multiple-item scale for measuring consumer perceptions of service quality. *Journal of Retailing, 64*(1), 12-37.

Rao, A. R., & Sieben, W. A. (1992). The effect of prior knowledge on price acceptability and the type of information examined. *Journal of Consumer Research, 19*(2), 256-270.

Saunders, J. A.; Hamilton, S. D., & Lancaster, G.A. (1978). A Study of variables Governing Choice of course in Higher Education. *Assessment in Higher Education, 6*(1), 61-75.

Schweitzer, A. M; Griffin, O.T; Ancis, J. R., & Thomas, C. R. (1999). Social Adjustment Experience of African American College Students. *Journal of Counselling Development, 7*(1), 189-197.

Selnes, F., & Troye, S. V. (1989). Buying expertise, information search, and problem solving. *Journal of Economic Psychology, 10*(3), 411-428.

Shultz, T. R., & Lepper, M. R. (1996). Cognitive Dissonance Reduction as Constraint Satisfaction. *Psychological Review, 103*(1), 219-240.

Shultz, T. R, Léveillé, E, & Lepper, M.R. (1999). Free Choice and Cognitive Dissonance Revisited: Choosing "Lesser Evils" Versus "Greater Goods". *Personality & Social Psychology Bulletin 1999*, 25, 40.

Singh, J. (2003). *Consumer Complaint Intentions and Behaviour.* Retrieved from http://www.sharjah.ac.ae/courseware/business_admin/syedaziz/consumer_behavior/presentations/Post-purchase%20Behaviour.pps.

Sojkin, B., Bartkowiak, P., & Skuza, A. (2012). Determinants of higher education choices and student satisfaction: the case of Poland. *Higher Education, 63*(5), 565-81.

Wells, V., & Daunt, K. (2011). *Eduscape: an exploratory analysis of the physical learning environment,* Proceedings of the Academy of Marketing Annual Conference 2011, Liverpool, 5-7 July 2011.

Wilkie, W. L. (2000). *Consumer Behaviour* (7th ed.). New York: John Wiley & Sons.

Wilkins, S., & Balakrishnan, M. S. (2013). Assessing student satisfaction in transnational higher education. *International Journal of Educational Management, 27* (2), 143-156.

Wilkins, S., & Epps, A. (2011). Student evaluation web sites as potential sources of consumer information in the United Arab Emirates. *International Journal of Educational Management, 25*(5), 410-422.

Chapter 4

Effectiveness of digital technology in teaching of literature in Kenyan universities: A case study of Pwani University

Remmy Shiundu Barasa,

Abstract

The 21st century has witnessed monumental growth in the use of digital communication in society. This has been manifested in science, business, farming, education, governance, medical care and art. Kenya has witnessed the most unprecedented growth in demand for university education in the East African region. Among the measures institutions of higher learning are putting in place to cope with increasing demand for higher education is a change in the method of delivery of content from the traditional face-to-face, to use of digital technologies. As such, digital technologies are now used at various levels with varying degrees of success. While studies exist that document the use of digital technology in teaching at institutions of higher learning, there is still a dearth of studies on its effectiveness among learners and more so in the field of literature in Kenya's universities. This study explores qualitative techniques to illuminate the experiences of Pwani University students in their learning of literature by way of digital technology. The results show that an increasing number of literature students are using digital technologies for more effective learning of the subject. The study makes policy and practical recommendations on the integration of digital technologies for learners of literature in institutions of higher learning.

Key words: Effectiveness, pedagogy, literature, new digital technology, Pwani University.

Introduction and Background

The last two decades have seen tremendous shift in pedagogical practices at all levels in the education sector (Siemens & Titternberger, 2009). At the centre of this epochal shift has been the revolutionary use of digital technologies especially the use of Internet. This has changed the traditional learning in higher education including the methods of course delivery, assessment, and other classroom activities. Oblinger (2004) notes that due to rapid technological innovations, learners have become digitally connected. They have also become hyperkinetic, adventurous, impatient, and highly collaborative. These learners prefer more stimulating, learner-centred learning experiences in which they enjoy and guide themselves. They also prefer less expensive learning resources that are easily accessible (Siemens & Titternberger, 2009). To adapt to the situation, learners in the higher learning institutions have been left with no other option other than to embrace the trending new technologies.

According to Boit and Kipkoech (2012) there has been a surge in demand for university education in Kenya, not comparable to elsewhere in the East African region. A large number of people are enrolling for university education today more than any other time in the past. Thus, the demand for university education continues to surpass the supply. Among the measures that universities have taken to cope with the situation is the adoption of digital learning. This involves the use of computer and network-enabled transfer of skills and knowledge. E-learning is preferred because it is flexible and suited to distance learning. There are several reasons why digital technology is the pedagogical method of choice. This mode of content delivery is considered beneficial to the users because it enables learners to access quality educational resources, equitable access to information and helps to nurture sharing of information; helps to bridge the gap between the learner and facilitator and ultimately improves the teaching methods and checks pressure on available resources; is flexible and readily accessible for as long as one is within internet connectivity. This bridges the gap between distance and the lecturer. Other characteristics of this mode of content delivery are that it leads to knowledge discovery as unexplained issues can easily be resolved through the web and collaboration with other internet users; ensures rapid and less costly distribution channels of educational materials and knowledge around the globe and; gives learners freedom to choose what to read, at what time, and at what pace.

Hollow and ICWE (2009) collaborate this information by arguing that digital technology is invaluable as it allows for human development which is necessary in the global economy as well as enabling lecturers to invest in more innovative teaching. The extent to which digital technologies have been adopted in institutions of higher learning in Kenya and Africa as a whole is still a matter that calls for detailed research (Thakrar, Zinn & Wolfenden, 2009). However, available literature suggests that in most parts of Sub-Saharan Africa, limited access to computers and related technologies due to poverty, lack of good communication networks, lack of power, language barriers, technical illiteracy, prejudices, and lack of government support may derail adoption of digital technologies.

In Africa, digital learning is taking root in Nigeria (Kamba, 2009), Tanzania (Ndume, Tilya & Twaakyondo, 2008), Uganda (Kasse & Balunywa, 2013), and Zimbabwe (Mpofu, Samukange & Kusure, 2012). In Kenya, a number of universities today have started digital learning programs, a measure considered to have a high likelihood of increasing accessibility to university education. This study, therefore, seeks to evaluate the status and effectiveness of digital learning in public universities in Kenya with specific focus on Pwani University. The chapter then highlights the opportunities that can be exploited to promote digital use in this university.

While some studies have been done to investigate technology integration in Kenyan higher learning institutions, most educationists, technology experts and other stakeholders are arguably appearing not to focus their attention on the experiences of learners (Hennessy, Onguko & Harrison, 2010). Therefore, the purpose of this qualitative study is to explore the reflections and experiences of learners who have integrated new digital technologies in their learning of literature in Pwani University. New digital technologies mean all the current digital innovations and software that include and not limited to social networks and media, open source, computers and web 2.0 that people engage for information sharing and communication (Agbatogun, 2013).

Research context

This study is set within a context of a technologically driven curriculum for the 21st century student in an African university. Using a case study of Pwani University, the author explores the effectiveness of digital technology in learning literature at the university level. The study illuminates the experiences, views and feelings of literature students as they embrace digital technology in their day to day learning and in other social activities.

The status of digital learning at Pwani University was assessed using the following criteria: availability of a digital learning policy to allow its systematic and structured use; level of awareness and utilization of digital learning among students; preferred methods of pedagogy by students and; finally, digital learning infrastructure and technologies utilized. Findings of this study revealed that adoption of digital learning is still at its infancy stage at Pwani University.

Digital learning policy is formulated to guide in the systematic utilization of online instruction methods in universities to ensure a structured content delivery. In spite of this, Pwani University did not have a clearly defined policy on digital learning leaving the whole matter to the discretion of the lecturer and their students. This was a major challenge in the adoption and utilization of digital learning at the university.

Kenya's national digital technology policy implemented in January 2006 aims at ensuring accessible, efficient, reliable, and affordable digital equipment services in the country. This policy promises that the Kenyan government will not only encourage but also invest in the use of information and communication technology in all its educational outlets including schools, colleges and universities in order to improve the quality of learning, as well as access to, formal education. In addition, the Kenya Education Sector Support Program (KESSP), established in 2005 by the Ministry of Education, emphasizes the mainstreaming of digital technology into the teaching and learning processes. Although digital technology has a huge presence in these institutions, a national e-learning education policy to guide its implementation remains a challenge as more endowed individual universities appear to pursue their own policies to adopt and implement this phenomenon on their campuses.

Research objectives

1. Identify the variety of digital technologies that students have integrated into their learning.
2. Investigate the reasons why learners utilize the digital technologies they have chosen.
3. Discuss the learners' experiences and reflections on the effectiveness of learning literature using digital technology.
4. Identify the new digital technologies that learners recommend to be incorporated in their pedagogical activities to make their learning of literature more effective and enjoyable.
5. Recommend policy and practice on integration of digital technology in the learning and teaching of literature.

Research questions

1. What digital technologies have students integrated into their learning of literature at Pwani University?
2. Why do learners use the digital technologies they have chosen?
3. What are the learners' experiences and reflections on learning of literature using digital technology?
4. What new digital technologies do learners recommend for integration into their pedagogical activities by lecturers to make learning of literature more effective and enjoyable?
5. What policies and practices are necessary to make the integration of digital technologies in the teaching and learning of literature effective?

Review of literature

Technology is at the centre of rapid socioeconomic development. Hennessey et al. (2010) argue that it is because of acquisition of advanced technologies that China and India vented themselves out of their economic doldrums in a generation. They further argue that even across Europe and North America, technology maintained the West's economic, social, cultural, political, and military leadership. Despite all these innovative strides elsewhere, Africa was perceived as lagging behind in technological pursuits. But today, as technology spreads across Africa, innovative methods of utilizing technology are transforming almost every sphere of life (Hennessey et al., 2010).

According to West and Bleiberg (2013) digital technologies will play a central role in Africa's educational development, providing equal access to quality learning regardless of place, gender, and age. It will help the population to overcome urban/rural education gaps by allowing learning materials, resources, and student communication to travel long distances, creating an environment of interactive learning. Digital technologies will also help Africa move toward "Education for All"—a key United Nations Sustainable Development Goal, of offering timeless access to materials and extending learning outside the school building (United Nations, [UN], 2013). Digital technologies can help learners fill the void of a largely dysfunctional education sector by delivering high quality and reliable content for learners and teachers—empowering low income learners to access high quality education for posterity.

Use of digital technologies such as the internet and mobile computer devices such as smartphones and tablets has exponentially revolutionized pedagogical approaches in the field of education. West and Bleiberg (2013) state that development of digital learning technologies is a relatively new aspect to the academic and educational system as far as curriculum implementation is concerned. The main purpose of applying this mode of knowledge transfer is to ensure sustainable learning which in turn promotes and enhances effective pedagogy, teaching and learning methods (West & Bleiberg, 2013).

West and Bleiberg (2013) and Jacqui (2015) argue that curriculum content, teaching and learning practices are presented through social computing systems. They define digital learning as the administering of education and teaching by way of integrating information communication technology, internet and enterprise cloud computing systems. They argue that technology has bolted out of the laboratories where it was conceived and stormed into classrooms with immense effect on teaching and learning practices. These digital technologies have led to infinite opportunities of education to learners and their lecturers. The lecturers and students can easily access information and knowledge resources from anywhere and at any time of their choice through the various digital technology outlets.

Zaman, Shamim & Clement (2011) state that digital technology learning practices include a number of technological communication devices such as mobile computer devices and the internet among other e-learning resources. In order to achieve efficiency with regard to digital learning in higher education in Kenya, the student should have the necessary competencies and intellectual insights in the use of technological communication facilities (Kandiri, 2012). Due to their rising popularity, digital learning devices are some of the most rapidly growing learning resource areas of teaching in education.

However, Kenyan government strategies to actualize digital learning technologies have been dragged behind by several educational institutions which do not effectively embrace the digital platforms. In this case, research has shown that in most universities, the traditional content delivery methodologies continue unchanged as the technology remains underutilized in the lecture halls. Actualization of digital technologies in universities is a challenging process that requires the fundamental digital solutions, the know-how and relevant competencies together with supportive and favourable administrative, financial and curriculum reconstitution (Zaman et al., 2011).

Status of e-learning in African universities

Several studies have been done on status of digital learning in universities in Africa. Hollow and ICWE (2009) reported on a survey of 147 digital learning consumers from a sample of 34 countries in Africa. It was reported that digital learning was still developing although the number of lecturers trained on how to use it was discouraging. There were also budgetary constraints to meet the cost of internet usage and other digital learning infrastructure.

Kamba (2009) examined the status of digital learning in 18 selected universities from different specialization areas in Nigeria. Findings of the study showed a high degree of awareness of digital learning among the universities. Despite this, he established that adoption of e-learning was poked down by a low level of funds allocation and lack of commitment by institutions to develop e-learning software. But of the two challenges, the lack of commitment was described as having been the worst according to the study. The most interesting thing was that most of the lecturers and their students in the universities used internet related e-learning sites mainly for searching information related to their research, since their resource centres and libraries could not provide them with the necessary materials. The study also found out that some of the universities had web pages that were mostly designed for public relations exercises but not for digital learning activities. The most encouraging thing, though, was that some of the universities planned to increase budgetary allocation to digital learning.

Mpofu et al. (2012) conducted a study in Zimbabwe which showed that the majority of the lecturers (97.5%) who facilitated open, distance and e-learning had no experience in distance education at all. Effective use of distance learning technologies demands that the lecturers be sufficiently trained in using distance education as a mode of academic delivery. The lack of knowhow is the challenge that continues to bestalk a good number of African scholars engaged in teaching in an online environment. This situation undermines efforts geared at introducing digital learning on the continent.

Walimbwa (2008) observes that despite digital learning growing at an unprecedented pace globally, East African universities were yet to fully maximize its potential. The study was undertaken at the University of Dar es Salaam, the University of Nairobi and at Makerere University. The study established that lack of skills and sufficient manpower was responsible for low digital learning implementation. Limited or lack of internet bandwidth and lack of policy harmonization were also notable factors that hindered digital learning from growing in these universities.

On their part, Kasse and Balunywa (2013) assessed the implementation of digital learning in Ugandan institutions of higher learning namely Makerere University; Makerere University Business School (MUBS); Kampala International University (KIU), and Islamic University in Uganda (IUIU). The choice of these institutions was based on the fact that they are the highest-ranking institutions in Uganda in terms of the quality of education, student population, and ICT adoption. Findings of their study showed that digital learning was used mostly as a means of delivering learning material (80%), minimally used to conduct discussions (12%) as well as to conduct assessment (2%). Their study revealed major infrastructural and technical incompetence, and attitudinal challenges (by lecturers and students) that limited full-scale adoption of digital learning in these institutions. Some of the infrastructural challenges included lack of electricity and unavailability of Internet connectivity.

A study conducted in some universities in Tanzania found that as is the case with other African countries, the implementation of digital learning was still very low despite the opportunities provided by the open source technology and the supportive environment created by the government (Sanga, Sife & Lwoga, 2007). The trio further found that among the ten universities studied; only the University of Dar es Salaam had managed to implement digital learning platforms such as WEBCT and Blackboard which are digital learning proprietary software. The other universities such as Sokoine University of Agriculture, Mzumbe University, and Open University of Tanzania possessed basic ICT infrastructure such as a local area network, Internet, computers, and CD and DVD facilities that formed the basis for the establishment of e-learning platform; but, the implementation of e-learning was minimal (Sanga, Sife & Lwoga, 2007).

Extensive research on the acceptance of digital learning in higher learning institutions in Tanzania identified several factors that challenged its implementation (Ndume et al., 2008). For example, the study identified lack of capacity analysis before online digital learning programmes as a major challenge facing its adoption in the country. A negative learning culture towards digital learning was also found to be another obstacle that impeded its implementation. Electricity power interruptions and inadequate ICT infrastructure for digital learning were also found to be major challenges. However, it was observed that there was an existing initiative by the government, private companies, and non-governmental organizations to improve ICT infrastructure. On the brighter side, the study revealed that reduction of taxes on computer items had enabled a good number of students to procure their own personal computers or laptops.

Nyerere, Gravenir & Mse (2012) carried out research on challenges that hindered the realization of digital learning in Kenya. Using the case of Kenyatta University and the University of Nairobi, the study established that universities faced various challenges in mounting this digital form of learning. The identified challenges included non-optimal utilization of programme facilities, delays in production of learning resource material, low budgetary allocation and poor teaching staff preparedness were real challenges. The other key problem was that this form of digital learning in Kenya was not supported by national policies hence the challenge of resource mobilization and even issues related to quality assurance.

Another study in Kenya by Odhiambo (2009) compared the perception of digital learning in Jomo Kenyatta University of Agriculture and Technology and the United States International University. The researcher set out to establish learners' non-receptive attitude and therefore minimum use of digital learning by students in the two universities. The study showed that essential aspects of digital use for effective content delivery were not used optimally to realize full benefit of the programme. The lecturers' methodology was also found to be inappropriate.

Han and Lex (2010) stated that developing modern digital learning programmes called for more innovation and creativity beyond the mere digitalization of books and lecture notes. They further noted that the starting point in the development of any e-learning programme is the whole question of who teaches, who should be taught and what should be taught. This means that creating a learning culture has roots in a person's socialization process which in turn impacts on their behaviour change in order to perform. An effective learning process demands that the learners own the process and get actively involved.

Information communication technology has revolutionized various aspects of the socio-cultural and economic lives of people. ICT has particularly registered its indelible presence in banking, engineering, medicine and media, among other sectors. However, its application in the education sector for pedagogical purposes remains behind. Many respondents indicated that e-learning is still an elusive and rare form of digital dispensation of curriculum delivery. An inquiry into specific e-learning approaches have yielded that there is still not a particular competency to exclusively write about.

Digital technologies in Kenya's universities

Inhabited by almost 41 million residents, Kenya is one of Africa's fastest growing countries in regard to telecommunications infrastructure. Together with South Africa, Nigeria and Egypt, Kenya plays a critical role in driving innovations across the continent (Boit & Kipkoech, 2012). Kenya is a lot more proactive within the telecommunications industry than one would think, and from the statistics available, it is clear that the country has a passion for implementing its information and telecommunications agenda.

According to Boit and Kipkoech (2012) Kenya is Africa's fourth largest country in terms of Internet users with a total of 11 million by close of 2011. Nations ranked ahead of Kenya are Nigeria (45 million), Egypt (21.7 million) and Morocco (15.7 million). South Africa is positioned below Kenya with 6.8 million of its people using the Internet (Boit & Kipkoech, 2012). Kenya's 11 million users accessing the Internet represent 25 percent of the population. Of this number, 1.2 million Kenyans actively use Facebook. The use of internet in Kenya has boomed since the turn of the 21st century. Boit and Kipkoech (2012) argue that in the year 2000, for instance, only about two hundred thousand people accessed and used the internet. The rapid rise, thereafter, can be attributed to lower internet costs and the subsequent introduction of undersea cables to the East African region as well as reliable and widespread electricity connectivity.

Gudo, Olel, and Oanda (2011) argue that the average age of the 11 million citizens accessible to the internet ranged between 15-34 years old, while 21 percent of this age bracket belonged to the 18-24 age brackets. About 60 percent of the Internet users were post-primary educated who spent more than one hour on the Internet per visit. The most popular online activities in Kenya were entertainment games and music social networking. Others were instant messaging, e-mails, general surfing and job search. Besides, Kenya had the second most active Twitter user base in Africa, with 2.4 million users (Gudo et al., 2011). South Africa has the highest number of Twitter users with over 5 million, while Nigeria has only 1.6 million and Egypt 1.2 million (Gudo et al., 2011).

Using technology to engage in international development is difficult in a region where the Internet has not reached every sector of the population (Kamba, 2009). Creative talent, curiosity, and innovative entrepreneurial spirit have helped shape the Kenyan technology community. Kenya's information technology project provides a platform for the African community to establish technological connectivity by harnessing the power of community organization and information technology. The two technology aid organizations, *iHub* and *Ushahidi*, are at the forefront of technology-led community engagement in Kenya (Kamba, 2009).

One of the first African information technology systems began with the launching of *Ushahidi* (Swahili word for 'testimony') in 2008 during the post-election violence. Based in Kenya, *Ushahidi* was basically software developed by volunteers such as media practitioners, software engineers, and community supporters who sought to increase information access and transparency by use of innovative software applications. This general experience in the use of information technology was potentially relevant in launching specific digital programmes such as the e-learning for Kenya's educational sector. But does e-learning influence the learners' performance? Scholars who have attempted to answer this question have done so at both the theoretical and empirical levels but still they have faced the challenge of measuring the student's performance and attribute it solely to the digital learning and not other important influences such as environment (Kulik, 1994; Atwell & Battle, 1999; Sosin, et al., 2004; Woessman, 2004).

The role of e-learning in students' achievement

The conventional approach to this phenomenon identifies achievement and curricula; how the learner understands the courses and the scores they get as key indicators of performance (Kulik 1994). However, a more extensive definition deals with competencies, skills and attitudes learned through the education experience. Woessman (2004) states that the simple definition enables the observation of the effects of any variation in higher education, while the in-depth definition needs a more intricate strategy of observation and a focus on the job market. The outcomes of education are foremost collaborated in the labour market.

The relationship between the use of digital technologies and student performance in higher education is not clear, and there are contradictory results in the literature review. The first explanation is that most of the literature has focused on direct effects of digital technology while it is more appropriate to examine the indirect impact through the long-established channels. Since student achievement is primarily determined by a student's behaviour, educational environment and the tutors' behaviour, digital technology may have an effect on these variables and consequently the output of education. Woessman (2004) argues that the differences noted in the performances of students are therefore more related to the differentiated effect of digital technology on the standard determinants. The other assumption is that information communication technology requires a modification in organisation. While information and communication technology tools and use frequencies are growing quite fast elsewhere in the world such as the West, the implementation of matching organizational packages is notably slow in Africa and varies from one institution to another. This may explain the observed variations in students' performance.

Kulik's (1994) reveals that students who got involved in digital-based instruction scored higher than those who did not use computers. The students also learned more content in comparatively less time and enjoyed their classes more when digital-based instruction was included. Sosin et al. (2004) discovered low positive effect on student performance due to digital use. But the researchers demonstrated that some digital use appeared to be encouragingly correlated to performance while others did not. Fuchs and Woessman (2004) explored international data from the Programme for International Student Assessment which revealed that while the bivariate correlation between the accessibility to digital use and students' performance was strongly and notably positive, the correlation became small and inconsequential when other student environment behaviours were considered.

An examination of the impact of these methodological and technological discoveries on the students' motivations towards the learning process and on students' achievement appeared to be mutating towards a consensus. Accordingly a suitable use of digital innovations in tertiary education could impact positively both on students' attitude and on their performance. Attwell and Battle (1999) analysed the relationship between having a computer at home for students' studies and school performance, for a sample of about 65,000 students in the United States. The researchers found that students, who had access to a home computer for educational studies, had better scores in reading and arithmetic.

Coates et al. (2004) reveal that students enrolled in on-campus courses performed better than their online counterparts though this variation is insignificant. Li, Leboeuf and Basu (2003) assert that since web-based instruction presents learning materials in a non-linear style, it allows students to discover new information through browsing and cross-referencing activities. Again, web-based instruction enhances active learning processes supported by constructivist theory. Web-based education also reinforces understanding through rejuvenated visualization. It is also convenient and could be used any time, at any place.

The role of e-learning in Literature

The use of digital technology to teach literary texts can be an opportunity of priceless authentic motivation, cultural and language enrichment. This pedagogical device can also develop in personal involvement that enhances individual student performance. In addition, literature can be enjoyable and motivating material that can help learners to develop their interpretative and analytical skills as well as their research abilities. Some studies have shown how the use of digital equipment in the teaching of literature such as the use of e-mail (Meskill & Ranglova, 2000; Jackstadt & Müller-Hartmann, 2001), multimedia (Yeh, 2005), and the internet (King, 2000; Schaumann, 2001) reinforce the learning of the target language. Although most of these studies show typical uses of technology, there remains a paucity of research focusing on the impact of technology on the teaching and learning literature in Kenya's universities. Paran (2006) recommends more research investigating the methods used in teaching literature within specific contexts of language and countries.

Methodology

This study employs qualitative research techniques which rely solely on the collection of non-numerical data such as words and pictures (Cresswell, 2013; Johnson & Christensen, 2012). Generally, this study is explorative in nature as it studies the phenomenon in a natural setting by investigating perspectives and views of a group of people on the integration of technology at Pwani University. The literary texts taught included novels, plays, poetry, short stories and oral literature as prescribed by the corresponding course outlines.

Research site, population, and participants

The research site for this study was Pwani University in Kenya. The population involved in this study included Pwani University's literature in English students, lecturers, ICT staff, and administrative staff. Due to time limit, this study managed to recruit thirty two (32) participants: fifteen (15) second year literature students (7 female and 8 male); six (6) third year literature students (3 female and 3 male); six (6) fourth year literature students (3 female and 3 male); three (3) lecturers (two male and one female); one (1) ICT staff; and an administrator (1). The participating students represented 10 percent of their class population whereas the lecturers represented 25 percent of the lecturers who taught literature at Pwani University. These participants had ranging knowledge and experience in the use of digital technology for different purposes like in learning and teaching, accessing and sharing information, socialization and entertainment.

Sampling strategies

Multiple sampling strategies were employed to recruit a suitable sample for this study. The first sampling strategy employed was the purposive sampling strategy in which the researcher specified the target population and then identified a few students who were suitable to the study (Johnson & Christensen, 2012). The characteristics that were considered in this research were being a higher learning student of literature, and being at least a second year undergraduate student. First year students were not considered for this study because their short duration at the university could not have given them a full understanding of the University's teaching and learning, based on just a few classes they had taken since they were admitted.

The second sampling strategy employed in this study was convenience sampling, in which the researcher included the students who were available and willing to participate in the study (Johnson & Christensen, 2012). The third sampling strategy was the snowballing sampling in which the researcher used formerly recruited participants to identify one or more additional people, who met the stated characteristics and were available to participate in the study (Johnson & Christensen, 2012).

Data collection

Primary data was collected using three research tools: questionnaire, in-depth interviews, and focused group discussions (FGD). Two separate structured questionnaires were designed and self-administered to second, third and fourth year students of literature at Pwani University. Through the interviews, additional insights on challenges affecting adoption of digital learning were collected. Three FGDs each with a maximum number of 11 people were held. The selection criteria also took into consideration the various diversities and interests in the university such as gender, regional balance and age. The information collected through the FGDs and in-depth interviews was used to corroborate data collected using the questionnaires. In depth interviews, on the one hand, were used because they were open-ended and had discovery method aspect which enabled the researcher to explore the respondents' feelings and perspectives on the subject of the research. Questionnaires, on the other hand, enabled the researcher to collect a lot of information from a big number of people at a relatively low cost within a short time. Research documents—both soft and hardcopies—such as books, periodicals, magazines, theses and conference papers obtained through the internet and libraries were analysed to review the literature on the status and effectiveness of e-learning.

Data analysis

The data was collected, coded and the various responses generated in the interviews, questionnaires and focused group discussions were grouped and arranged in accordance to the research questions. The data were then put under various descriptive topics. The researcher then engaged in content analysis of the information received from participants. The analysis was then presented in descriptive form.

Results

The digital learning technologies are a familiar concept among students in Pwani University although the students did not have any special training for e-learning. The outcome of this study indicated that digital learning is still emerging as an alternative and complementary pedagogical approach at the University. Interviews with key personnel in the University revealed that the university did not have senate approved digital technologies learning policies to guide the implementation of digital pedagogical methods.

Findings of this study revealed that while digital learning technologies were used by students, it was not as widespread as expected. It was revealed that 20 percent of the lecturers used e-learning techniques while 80 percent did not. The majority of lecturers preferred traditional methods. Kandili (2012) and Ayele et al. (2010) argue that for effective and sustainable e-learning, lecturers must be well trained and knowledgeable. Many students still used traditional methods of learning. The reasons adduced to this preference were ease of reference to hard copies; lack of ICT skills on how to use digital technologies and; lack of appropriate equipment.

Results showed that not only the participants were familiar with a number of digital tools useful for learning, but they also owned one or more devices and used them for different purposes. The data shows that students were familiar with the new digital technologies, but that they had diverse experience in the technologies that they use and own. All students knew some common digital devices like desktop computers, laptops, tablets (iPad), and smartphones. When asked about the social network they knew, Facebook and WhatsApp were instantly mentioned followed by Twitter. They were also familiar with Skype, blogs and Google+; although some of those social networks came up when students were responding to follow up questions. Most of the students owned laptops, and smartphones and some even had tablets.

All students in this study had accounts with varied number of social networks, and they spent different amount of time on these social networks depending on the number and kind of people with whom they were connected. The students said that they used Facebook and WhatsApp to make connections with friends. They also spent quite a considerable amount of time on WhatsApp and

Facebook since the two platforms are connected to global system for mobile communication (GSM) networks for most of the time.

Discussion

Viewed from the channels of diffusion of innovations as expressed by Rogers (1995), it appears that the university is at the early stage of adoption during which most people and organizations are not yet convinced about the usefulness of the innovation and are indecisive as to whether to adopt it or not.

Yet, as shown in the literature review, Kenya is not the only country where digital learning is still at its infancy. Other countries in Africa such as Nigeria, Tanzania, and Uganda are also grappling with challenges of low adoption of this mode of learning (Mpofu et al., 2012). Students had varied responses on why they used digital technologies they had chosen for learning. Searching for resources was one of the main reasons. One participant, the administrator, believed that students used laptops only, and not other devices, for searching online resources. He said, 'although some students do not possess laptops, they are always surfing in cyber cafes or on their smartphones. He also said that who did not have laptops or smartphones of their own 'borrowed laptops from their friends, when they wanted to search for online materials'.

Students agreed that they used laptops and desktop computers for online resources. One of them said, 'I could easily get what I want to study, and get materials which go beyond what lecturers present in classrooms'. Another student reported that 'it is very easy to get books and articles online which has helped me to understand better what my lecturers teach.' Another student observed that 'our library does not always have the course recommended books so I resort to the internet to access those books.'

Connection and collaboration was another reason. Although social networks for connection and socialization may be considered non-academic, results show that some students used them for communicating academic matters, especially, WhatsApp for carrying out group assignments. Several students and their lecturers reported that lecturers sent assignments to class representatives through

WhatsApp for onward transmission to other students. One student participant who happened to be a class representative said, 'whenever lecturers miss classes they opt to send assignments on my WhatsApp so that I share such tasks with the rest of the class.' However, it seems that students preferred the traditional face-to-face as their collaborative method.

The other reason was creation and presentation. Students used laptops and desktop computers for creating and presenting learning materials in classrooms. While they also used the internet for searching for resources that they shared with fellow students and assignments, they also used the same for creating group assignments and making class presentations.

Students did not have many tools to recommend. This could be due to the fact that they were not well-informed about how technology can work so powerfully in teaching and learning. Their background in curriculum design and educational technology was more theoretical than practical to enable them see potentialities of technology in learning. They, however, made the following recommendations: Students advocated for more use of web tools for searching online resources. They showed that search engines such as Google could be well utilized, and students could be inducted on how to use them effectively to get the most out of it. One student said, 'majority of us have smartphones and interact widely on Facebook and WhatsApp, an idea that makes web 2.0 the best platform to launch e-learning programmes.' Some students suggested that this was important because most of the academic materials were found from strong internet engines like Google where someone can download a book/article.

Results show that students suggested the use of online videos. One student observed, 'YouTube videos, if integrated, would be fascinating in learning. This is because YouTube videos can help us understand a lot of things.' There are good instructional videos that can be used in classroom. However, the concern was whether the internet would be sufficient to stream those videos.

One of the students advocated for integration of social networks in content delivery. This student recommended 'integration of as much social networks as available.' He mentions in particular

Facebook, WhatsApp, Skype, and blogs (web 2). The student said, 'I truly use a lot of time on Facebook and WhatsApp. If there was a way lecturers integrated their assignments with this new communication platform, I could real do a lot in my academic work.' One of the lecturers agreed with the student's idea. The lecturer thought that the advent of social media had swept away a whole generation of young people including university students and that pedagogical approaches needed to be revised to accommodate this phenomenal change. Said the lecturer, 'with the government's commitment towards free education for all at all levels, I'm confident that students who come from poor backgrounds would not be left out due to the expenses that come with digital devices.' The lecturer thought that 'students should be encouraged to buy the devices and use them for their own leaning purposes.'

Although the use of digital technologies is evident among lecturers and students, results show that their integration in learning and instructions is still minimal. Lecturer participants did not provide information that shows adequate use of the available technologies. The only technologies that the three lecturers and students made use of were laptops, the internet, and projectors. They used their laptops to search for online resources. One of the lecturers said, I use my laptops to prepare my Power Point slides, ready for presentation by using a projector.' Participants in this study had unknowingly already integrated a few of these digital technologies in their studies/teachings. They had also seen how technological integration facilitates learning. However, lecturers had not used Skype for giving feedback to students—a situation that explains why they need to utilize the idea. Siemens and Titternberger (2009) emphasize the need to give learners immediate and timely feedback.

Another important thing is that since most students use laptops and smartphones for downloading online resources, lecturers have the opportunity to assign them with online activities other pedagogical activities in literary works that would help them to understand the content even better. As one of the students suggested, 'I would like to see his instructors assigning him some instructional activities that could be accomplished by using the tools he already has.

Another open opportunity would be utilizing free online sharing tools such as Google Drive, Box, Dropbox, Sky Drive, One Drive etc. and share them with other students. The abundance of self-directed search for online resources could be utilized by asking students to upload the materials in shared online folders or resource wikis. This would make students become co-creators/co-authors of the learning materials. Lecturers could also ask their students to create online portfolios of resources they get online and share them with their classmates in order to facilitate collaboration among students.

Social network groups, like WhatsApp and Facebook groups can be created for particular classes to allow sharing of different resources. These social media make a practical tool for sharing information, exchanging ideas, debating issues and sharing videos, pictures and other mediated resources for each student to utilize. Many of the free YouTube videos which would be useful in different learning contexts could be shared on these social networks. This can help students to come to class well prepared and aware of the content of previous and oncoming lessons. Lecturers could also use these tools to disseminate information and announcements related to their courses and programmes.

Participants in this study complained that their learning institutions lacked enough technological equipment for all the faculty and students. As participants said, there were no enough functioning computers in lecturer offices and students' computer labs. 'It is high time that the Kenyan universities see the importance of investing in the future of their students through digital learning,' said one student participant. For Vision 2030 to be realized, the government must practically fund the learning environment of its universities.

The data also showed that lack of tech-know-how among lecturers and students, power outages, high costs of internet, and unreliable internet are still the main challenges that hinder technology integration at the University's learning classrooms. It appeared like lecturers still had a limited understanding of the kinds and ways of using different digital technologies for teaching and learning. Participants, for instance, were well aware of the digital devices and social networks which were used for other purposes like sharing information, entertainment, and socialization, but they had a limited knowledge of how these tools could be used for instructional purposes. It seemed there were hardly any technological seminars and in-service courses available for lecturers at the University. Kajuna (2009) argues that workshops for lecturers may well help to remedy the situation, for; the lecturers come to learn how to provide their students with technology-based instructions which would help them to enjoy learning.

Conclusion

Although a lot of challenges still persist in Kenya's use of technology due to factors like lack of power and lack of adequate equipment, opportunities for integrating new digital technologies in universities still exist. The existing opportunities for integrating new digital technologies such as mobile devices and social networks are not adequately utilized. If properly utilized, digital technologies could make Kenya's university education enjoyable and highly fruitful. Although the government has not invested enough in educational technology by financing purchase of sufficient technological equipment, lecturers and students could still utilize the existing technological setting to a better level.

There are many students with smartphones, laptops and other devices that can be put to good use in e-learning. The overall findings of this study revealed that Pwani University has not yet fully adopted e-learning as a mode of content delivery and has not made significant strides in that direction. There was no evidence of senate approving e-learning policies which hampered a uniform and structured adoption of e-learning at the University. In addition, the low percentage of lecturers and students using digital learning hints at the fact that e-learning at public universities in Kenya is still at its formative stage. In the case of Pwani University, there was little evidence of modules uploaded for the students' use. There was no evidence of the learning management systems where such modules would be uploaded and any attempted effort in that direction yielded low quality modules that lacked in interactivity. The digital learning infrastructure and capacity in the University is still insufficient in terms of digital skills and availability of enough functioning computers.

Recommendations

Arising from the findings of this study, the following recommendations if implemented will lead to improvement of e-learning in public universities in Kenya:

- All university senates should approve and fast track digital learning policies
- Lecturers should be motivated and trained to use e-learning in their subject areas in a more interactive and effective way.
- Lecturers should be encouraged to integrate their teaching with e-learning by preparing both online and offline teaching materials and content. The materials prepared offline could be uploaded when ready.
- Computer courses should be compulsory at all levels of both undergraduate and graduate studies.
- As a condition for admission, students should have a laptop, a tablet or a good smartphone. The government and university management could easily bring the private sector on board to ensure this.
- Each university should establish technical support staff at disciplinary level to continuously prepare and package course content in a more interactive and motivating manner.
- The Ministry of Education should develop clear e-learning policies and guideline to ensure every university implements the policy.
- The government and universities should give budgetary allocations to e-learning in the universities to target improvement of digital infrastructure, research, capacity building, and attitude management and create awareness.

References

Agbatogun, A. (2013). Interactive digital technologies' use in Southwest Nigerian Universities. *Education Tech Research Dev* 61, 333 – 35.

Attwell, P. & Battle, J. (1999). Home Computers and School Performance. *The Information Society.* 15, pp. 1-10.

Boit, J., & Kipkoech, L. (2012). Liberalization of higher education in Kenya: Challenges and prospects. *International Journal of Academic Research in Progressive Education and Development, 1*(2), 33–41.

Coates, D., & Humphreys, B. (2004). No Significant Distance between face-to-face and online instruction: Evidence from principles of Economics. *Economics of Education Review*, 23(6) 533-546.

Creswell, J. (2012). *Educational research: Planning, conducting, and evaluating quantitative and qualitative research* (4th ed.), MA: Pearson.

Daniels, J. (2000). Forward in information and communication technology in education. *A Curriculum for Schools and Programme for Teacher Development*, Paris, UNESCO.

Fuchs, T., & Woessmann, l. (2004). Computers and student learning: Bivariate and multivariate evidence on the availability and use of computers at home and at school. *CESifo Working Paper*, No. 1321, November, Munich.

Gudo, C., Olel, M.A., & Oanda, O. (2011). University expansion in Kenya and issues of quality education: Challenges and opportunities. *International Journal of Business and Social Science, 2*(20), 203–214.

Hennessy, S., Onguko, B., Harrison, D., Ang'ondi, E.K., Namalefe, S., Naseem, A. & Wamakote, L. (2010). Developing the use of information and communication technology to enhance teaching and learning in East African schools: Review of the literature. *Research Report No. 1. Centre for Commonwealth Education & Aga Khan University.* Institute for Educational Development–Eastern Africa.

Hollow, D. & ICWE. (2009). *E-Learning in Africa: Challenges, priorities and future direction.*

Jackstadt, H., & Müller-Hartmann, A. (2001). Encounters: The virtual in search of the Intercultural. In J. Edge (Ed.), *Action research* (pp. 117-128), Alexandria, VA: TESOL.

Johnson, B., & Christensen, L. (2012). *Educational research, qualitative, quantitative and mixed approach.* (4th ed). California: SAGE Publication.

Kamba, M. (2009). Problems, challenges and benefits of implementing e-learning in Nigerian universities: An empirical study. *International Journal of Emerging Technologies in Learning,* 4(1), 66–69.11.

Kandiri, M. (2012). *A survey on ICT access and use in Kenya secondary schools.* Nairobi: Summit Strategies.

Kasse, J., & Balunywa, W. (2013). *An assessment of e-learning utilization by a section of Ugandan universities: Challenges, success factors and way forward.* Paper presented at the International Conference on ICT for Africa 2013, Harare, Zimbabwe.

King, L. (2000). Teaching German literature through the web: Processes and outcomes. *Die Unterrichtspraxis,* 33(1), 61-70.

Li, Y., Leboeuf, E., Basu, P., & Turner, L. (2003). Development of a web-based mass transfer processes laboratory: System development and implementation. *Computer Applications in Engineering Education.* 11(1), 67-74.

Makori, E. (2012). Bridging the information gap with the patrons in university libraries in Africa: The case for investments in web 2.0 systems. *Library Review,* 61(1): pp. 30-40.

Meskill, C. & Ranglova, K. (2000). Sociocollaborative language learning in Bulgaria. In M. Warschauer & R. Kern (Eds.), *Network-based language teaching: Concepts and practice.* Cambridge: Cambridge University Press.

Ministry of Education, (2005). *Kenya Education Sector Support Program* (KESSP), 2005-2010.

Mpofu, V., Samukange, T., Kusure, L., Zinyandu, T., Denhere, C., Huggins, N. & Sithole, F. (2012). Challenges of virtual and open distance science teacher education in Zimbabwe. *International Review of Research in Open and Distributed Learning,* 13(1), 207-219.

Ndume, V., Tilya, F., & Twaakyondo, H. (2008). Challenges of adaptive e-learning at higher learning institutions: A case study in

Tanzania. *International Journal of Computing and ICT Research*, 2(1), 47–59

Nyerere, J., Gravenir, F., & Mse, G. (2012). Delivery of open, distance and e-learning in Kenya *International Review of Research in Open and Distributed Learning*, 13(3), 185–205.

Oblinger, D. (2004). The next generation of educational engagement. *Journal of Interactive Media in Education*, 2004 (1).

Odhiambo, O. (2009). Comparative study of the e-learning platforms used in Kenyan universities: Case study of Jomo Kenyatta University of agriculture and technology and United States International University. Unpublished MSC thesis, Strathmore University.

Paran, A. (2006). The stories of literature in language learning. In A. Paran (Ed.), *Literature in language teaching and learning* (pp.1-10). Alexandria, VA: TESOL.

Sanga, C., Sife, A. & Lwoga, E. (2007). New technologies for teaching and learning: Challenges for higher learning institutions in developing countries, *International Journal of Education and Development using Information and Communication Technology (IJEDICT)*, 3(2), 57–67.

Siemens, G. & Tittenberger, P. (2009). *Handbook of emerging technologies for learning*, University of Manitoba, Manitoba.

Sosin, K., Blecha, B., Agawal, R., Bartlett, R., & Daniel, J. (2004). Efficiency in the Use of Technology in Economic Education: Some Preliminary Results. *American Economic Review*, 94(2), 253-258.

Thakrar, J., Zinn, D. & Wolfenden, F. (2009). Harnessing Open Educational Resources to the Challenges of Teacher Education in Sub-Saharan. *International review of research in open and distance learning volume 10, number 4. ISSN: 1492-3831*.

United Nations. (2013). Transforming our World: The 2030 Agenda for Sustainable Development Goals, Sessional Paper.

Walimbwa, M. (2008). *Integrating e learning in teaching and research in upcoming East African regional Universities*, Paper presented at the meeting CNIE Banff, Alberta, Canada.

West, D., & Bleiberg, J. (2015). Education Technology Success Stories, *Centre for Technology Innovation at Brookings*.

Yeh, A. (2005). Poetry from the heart, *English Today, 21*(1), 45-51.

Zaman, M., Shamim, R. & Clement, K., 2011, 'Trends and issues to integrate ICT in teaching and learning for the future world of education'. *International Journal of Engineering & Technology*, 11(3), 114-119.

Chapter 5

Postgraduate Certificate in Education students' perspectives about learning using Blackboard at a university in South Africa.

Lawrence Meda

Abstract

The use of Blackboard has become so ubiquitous and widespread in institutions of higher learning in this 21st century. The platform is suitable for teaching in this era as it promotes student interaction and collaborative learning. There is a dearth of scholarship on research that focuses on the usage of Blackboard by students studying for short courses such as a Postgraduate Certificate in Education. The purpose of this research is to investigate Postgraduate Certificate in Education (PGCE) students' perspectives about learning using Blackboard at a university in South Africa. The study used a qualitative case study within an interpretivist paradigm. Sixteen students were purposively selected to complete open-ended questionnaires. The study found that although students are debilitated by poor internet connectivity on campus, they are enthusiastic about learning using the platform. It is concluded that Blackboard suits PGCE students' context and it is responsive to their needs and expectations of learning in the 21st century.

Key words: LMS; PGCE; Technology; University; Blackboard

Introduction and Background

Technology is increasingly being used to maximise student participation and engagement inside and outside lecture rooms in the 21st century. Higher education institutions around the world are progressively encompassing online modes of instruction (Bodey,

Ravaga & Sloan, 2016) to enhance teaching and learning in a cost effective way. Research shows that teaching using various technology which include online platforms does not only enhance the quality of learning, but also increases student retention (Leeds et al., 2013; Hamid, Waycott, Kurnia & Chang, 2015; Rambe & Bere, 2013).

Some students drop out of university education because of lack of money to travel to the learning institution for lectures. The use of an online Learning Management System (LMS) such as Blackboard assists in that context as students do not have to attend face-to-face lectures as often. Blackboard company (2006) postulates that LMSs do not only improve learning, but also recruitment and retention of students. The use of a LMS has successfully blurred a gap that exists between a lecturer and student, and distance education and campus-based experiences (Masi & Winer, 2005). The gap has been filled by web-based learning which knows no boundaries in higher education learning today.

The purpose of this research is to investigate PGCE students' perspectives about learning using Blackboard at a university in South Africa. There is a gap of research on PGCE students' perspectives about learning using Blackboard in South Africa, and a lack of knowledge in this area is what this study seeks to address. This chapter will firstly provide a brief definition of LMS and then present a deeply focused review of Blackboard which is the emphasis of this study. The PGCE curriculum will then be reviewed, along with a theoretical framework guiding this research. Methodology, results and discussion follow along with succinct conclusions.

The LMS and Blackboard

Although there is no single and universally accepted definition of LMS, Ellis (2009) defined it as a software application that automates the administration, tracking, reporting and delivery of training courses in education. The software is designed with the purpose of supporting student learning and it consists of numerous presentations, assessment, communication and management tools (Ellis & Calvo, 2007). Szabo and Flesher (2002) conceptualise LMS as a software that provides a platform for managing courses in a way that promotes student-centred learning. Despite the existence of several and sometimes differing definitions of the software, scholars unanimously agree that, in essence, a LMS is a web-based system which provides both instructors and students with multiple opportunities to easily gain access and share instructional materials online (Hussein, 2016; Kim & Do, 2016).

Watson and Watson (2007) summarised a LMS simply as a framework that manages all aspects of the learning process. It has unlimited possibilities of promoting student-centred learning and making interaction between all educational stakeholders easy (Isaias & Issa, 2013). One notable LMS which is used by many universities today is the Blackboard.

Although different LMSs are becoming ubiquitous technology which are being used to facilitate teaching in both traditional and open distance learning institutions in higher education, Blackboard is the most widely used web-based software. Blackboard is an emerging technology which is very resourceful and it is being used by many universities around the globe (Hamad, 2017; Kim and Do, 2016). Its main strength in education lies in its ability to enable student-centred learning which is credited as the most commendable way that ensures quality education. Student-centred learning is deeply rooted in constructivism. Constructivism is a Vygotsky (1978) theory which asserts that knowledge is a social construct brought about through interactions. It consists of knowledge acquisition and production by reiterating the fact that students have to be active participants in learning and making sense of their environment and their experiences within that setting (Deo, 2016).

Blackboard is a web-based application that affords students in the 21st century with unlimited opportunities to learn using the fundamentals that underpin constructivism. It (Blackboard) is an effective platform that enables lecturers to offer various ways of teaching which are typically student-centred (Pusuluri, Mahasneh & Alsayer, 2017). It enhances interactions among students themselves and between students and lecturers (Heirdsfield, Walker, Tambyah & Beutel, 2011).

Blackboard provides space for interactive engagement (Rambe, 2017), and it is ideal for collaborative learning in the 21st century. It is an integral tool that is being used to promote student interaction, communication, collaboration, and participation (Isaias & Issa, 2013). Pusuluri et al. (2017) maintain that the strength of Blackboard in higher education lies in its ability to provide a platform for interaction, collaboration and mediation. It enables students and instructors to have some form of flexibility, accessibility and convenience in the entire teaching and learning process (Hamad, 2017). Blackboard also increases staff productivity by accommodating numerous teaching and learning strategies which can be used to augment active learning in students (Heirdsfield et al., 2011).

Blackboard in higher education can be used to foster independent learning in an outcomes-based university (Lansari, Tubaishat & Al-Rawi, 2010). Its advantages in this digital era are innumerable. This is why Isaias and Issa (2013) summed up the use of Blackboard in higher education as a platform that creates a win-win situation. This assertion is in agreement with research conclusions made about the learning platform by scholars in different countries and universities.

In Saudi Arabia, Blackboard was recently introduced and it was viewed as an amazing technology which has brought significant changes in the country's universities (Hussein, 2016). A research conducted by Pusuluri et al. (2017) in Saudi Arabia found university students were contented with Blackboard as it offered a lively and interesting learning environment and variety in the learning of courses. Hamad (2017) concurs that university students in Saudi Arabia were satisfied with the collaborative nature of Blackboard as it enabled them to access and share downloaded learning materials any time they wanted. The learning platform is applauded in the Saudi Arabian context as a learning tool that is indispensable in terms of improving the teacher-student relationship and making learning easy and interesting all the time (Mohsin & Shafeeq, 2014).

In Australia, Heirdsfield et al. (2011) state that students praised Blackboard as it enabled them to access course content, library information and other materials such as homework and workshop activities posted by the lecturer at anytime and anywhere. Similarly, findings of a study of universities in Portugal and Australia concurred that uploading and submitting assessment tasks through Blackboard is more sustainable as it is cost-effective, practical and accessible (Isaias & Issa, 2013). Portugal's Open University student feedback showed that students were satisfied with the use of Blackboard as it was sustainable and interesting (Isaias & Issa, 2013). This corresponds with the way the platform is conceptualised in South Africa where it is believed to be a solid tool upon which effective teaching and learning rest (Kleinveldt, Schutte & Stilwell, 2016).

It is important to note that technology (in particular Blackboard) on its own is unable to facilitate teaching and learning. There is a need for an instructor to use it to enhance teaching and learning. This corresponds with the view of Microsoft's Bill Gates who said, "Technology is just a tool. In terms of getting the kids working together and motivating them, the teacher is the most important." The discussion forums on Blackboard increase students' interest and involvement, however that does not happen unless a lecturer facilitates. Academics have a responsibility of ensuring technology enhances students' learning not to just send information on Blackboard and conclude that the use of technology promotes students' interactive learning. This resembles the view of Deo (2016) who states that there is no substitute for a teacher in the teaching and learning process. Innovative use of digital technology such as Blackboard is there to assist the lecturer to make the entire teaching process more accessible in an effective and interactive way (Hamad, 2017; Deo, 2016). Blackboard needs to be used in all programmes offered in universities including the PGCE.

The PGCE Curriculum

In South Africa, PGCE is studied by people who have qualifications in fields other than education who want to become qualified teachers (DHET 2011; 2015). The qualification is offered as a professional teaching qualification to graduates with bachelor's degrees or equivalent diplomas. According to the Council on Higher Education [CHE] (2013, p. 42), "The Postgraduate Certificate in Education conforms to the specifications for an Advanced Diploma at NQF level 7, and the admission requirements, purpose and characteristics and progression opportunities for the PGCE are the same as those of the Advanced Diploma. However, due to the familiarity of the PGCE in international teacher education circles, the qualification will continue to be denoted by this title." The PGCE programme in many South African universities is offered full-time over one year or part-time over two years. It is pegged at the National Qualifications Framework (NQF) level 7 and has a minimum total credits of 120 which is equivalent to 1200 notional hours on the Higher Education Qualifications Sub-Framework (CHE, 2013; DHET, 2015).

The assumption underpinning the PGCE model in South Africa is that graduates training to become teachers already have the subject content knowledge of their discipline (Bertram, Mthiyane & Mukeredzi, 2013). However, they will be missing a teaching component which make them recognised qualified teachers. The PGCE comes to close this gap as it is aimed at equipping prospective classroom practitioners with specialised disciplinary knowledge and pedagogical skills which enables them to teach competently in schools (DHET, 2015; Bertram et al., 2013). This is responsive to a national policy on the Minimum Requirements for Teacher Education Qualifications (MRTEQ) which requires PGCE students to have an in-depth specialised knowledge and practical skills that should enable them to apply in schools in varying contexts (DHET, 2015).

The PGCE curriculum in South Africa allows students to study core education modules, teaching specialisation modules and teaching practice. Core education modules introduce students to various teaching theories of learning, classroom management strategies, curriculum studies and a wide range of teaching strategies (Bertram et al., 2013). Teaching specialisation allows students to focus on subjects which they will be teaching in schools. Teaching practice entails students going to schools to teach and they will be assessed by a university instructor and school mentor teacher (Nomlomo & Sosibo, 2016; Mukeredzi, Mthiyane & Bertram, 2015). The South African model of PGCE is more or less the same as the Scottish model, where student learning must take place in two very different contexts - the university and the placement schools (Christie, Conlon, Gemmell & Long, 2004).

Theoretical Framework

A theoretical framework guiding this study is Garrison, Anderson and Archer's (2000) Community of Inquiry (CoI). The origin of this theory can be traced back to the work of John Dewey, which is consistent with constructivist approaches to learning (Garrison & Arbaugh, 2007). Garrison et al. (2000) developed Dewey's idea of CoI and applied it to online learning contexts. The idea of CoI in an online learning context comes in the sense that there is evidence that a learning community can be created online where people can share information and learn best practices (Thompson & MacDonald, 2005; Shea, Li & Pickett, 2006). The CoI in an online context is made up of three fundamental elements: social presence, teaching presence and cognitive presence (Garrison & Arbaugh, 2007).

The social presence involves engagement of students with content using technology in order to achieve an educational goal that is set. This can be achieved when students are given online work to do in pairs and groups where they can interact and exchange different views about the subject. Students' collaboration with others and with lecturers gives rise to a social presence and a sense of online community (Garrison, 2011).

The cognitive presence involves the extent to which students are able to use their critical thinking skills to construct meaning (Garrison et al., 2001). Cognitive presence makes students deal with an educational problem using a systematic approach where they first identify the issue that requires inquiry, explore it as individuals or collaboratively, integrate new ideas and reach a resolution where a solution to the problem is applied in a real educational context (Garrison et al., 2001; Garrison & Arbaugh, 2007). Reflection is one of the important components of this cognitive presence because it enables students to use their thinking skills more effectively.

The teaching presence, as the words suggest, involves a teacher being part of the teaching and learning process. Technology on its own cannot facilitate students' learning. There is a need for teacher presence to direct students to use technology in order to learn. Garrison et al. (2000) argue that a combination of student interaction (social presence) and the use of critical thinking skills (cognitive presence) alone cannot promote effective online learning. There is a need for a teaching presence in order to direct students' interactions and learning (Garrison & Arbaugh, 2007). According to Garrison, Anderson and Archer (2001), the teaching presence is defined as 'the design, facilitation, and direction of cognitive and social processes for the purpose of realizing personally meaningful and educationally worthwhile learning outcomes.'

The three elements of CoI are interdependent as illustrated in Figure 1.

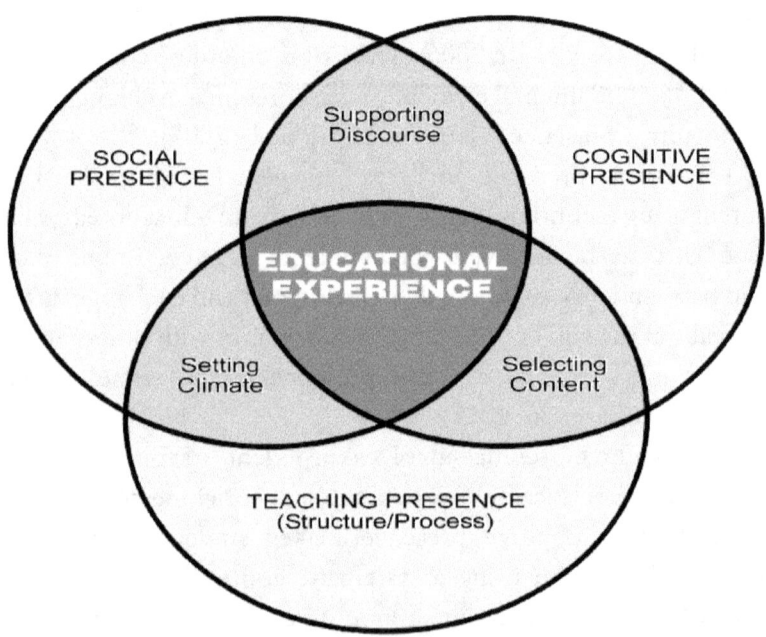

Figure 1. Community of Inquiry (Garrison 2011, p. 23)

Garrison, Anderson and Archer's theory of CoI is appropriate to guide this study because it has components that focus on students' interactions and teaching presence which are the basis of this research, where Blackboard is used to facilitate blended learning. A combination of the three components of CoI ensures a collaborative constructivist e-learning educational experience of students in the 21st century (Garrison, 2011). This corresponds with this research which looked at students' perspectives of their constructivist learning using an online platform - Blackboard - which is being used by universities today. The theory of CoI was also chosen as it has increasingly become popular in conceptualising learning using an online platform (Arnold & Ducate, 2006). Garrison and Arbaugh (2007) support the CoI as a parsimonious and coherent theory of studies that focus on teaching using the e-learning platform.

Methodology

This study was undertaken using a qualitative approach within an interpretivist paradigm. A qualitative approach was chosen because the researcher wanted participants to freely express their views in open-ended questionnaires. Creswell (2012) argues that a qualitative approach enables participants to freely express their ideas about a particular phenomenon. An interpretivist paradigm was preferred as it is compatible with a qualitative approach which aims at understanding a phenomenon under investigation (Neuman, 2011). Lapan, Quartaroli and Riemer (2012) argue that all qualitative research has an interpretive perspective which focuses on understanding and interpreting meaning of a phenomenon.

The study was done as a case study at a university of technology in South Africa. A case study was appropriate to use as it is usually used to increase the understanding of particular complex phenomena (Rahim & Chik, 2014). In this study, the phenomenon is understanding PGCE students' perspectives on learning using Blackboard. PGCE was deliberately selected because there is dearth of scholarship on learning using Blackboard at that level of study. The majority of studies which were undertaken about students' perspectives of Blackboard focused on undergraduate students. Data was collected using an open-ended questionnaire. An open-ended questionnaire was ideal to use as it allowed participants to freely write their views about the topic.

Sixteen PGCE students were purposively selected to participate in the study. Only 16 participants were selected because the study was done using a qualitative approach which uses small numbers (Cohen,

Manion & Morrison, 2007) in order to obtain rich textual data (Creswell, 2012). In this study, 'purposive sampling', a qualitative sampling procedure which allows the researcher to deliberately select participants and research techniques, was used (Creswell, 2012). Purposive sampling was preferred as it is adopted in almost all qualitative research where researchers use their judgment to select a sample that they believe, based on prior information, will provide the data they need (Fraenkel & Wallen, 2007). Purposive sampling was also chosen because criteria for sampling in case studies are usually purposeful with an emphasis on those cases that seem to offer opportunities to learn (Hall, Scott & Borsz, 2008).

Data was analysed using content analysis. Ethical issues were observed by informing participants about the purpose of the study. Participation was voluntary and all students had freedom to withdraw from the study at any point in time. Confidentiality was maintained throughout the study. Pseudonyms were used to enhance the participants' privacy.

Results

Results of this study show that PGCE students are very keen to learn using Blackboard. They liked Blackboard mainly because it is accessible and very convenient for them to use. It allows them to access learning information anywhere and at any time as was said by one student:

> I like using Blackboard because it allows me to view different learning materials in my own time, go through notes from class in my spare time and do things at my own pace. I really enjoy the convenience of using Blackboard anywhere and anytime.

Similarly, two other students reiterated the same view: "I enjoy learning using Blackboard simply because I am able to access it from anywhere, at my own time and it is easy to upload assignments"; "Blackboard gives you access to your academia in the comfort of your home." The learning platform is applauded by PGCE students mainly because of the advantage of enabling them to work in their own time and anywhere, including their homes. The learning platform does not only present advantages to students alone, but also lecturers, as was stated by one participant:

> I think Blackboard is the best option to use in higher education today because it is easy to use and every student can access it. It is also easy for lecturers to post learning materials to all students rather than using the email system.

Students preferred material to be communicated to them via Blackboard which is very easy for the lecturer as opposed to typing each and every students' email address. A student said:

> I think lecturers who do not use Blackboard do not have knowledge of the platform. This is evidenced by ways in which they prefer to send resources such as slides to us. One lecturer used an email system where he had to manually type all 90 students' email addresses in order to send the material to us. Such a laborious process would have been avoided by simply uploading the material on Blackboard and asking students to access in their own time.

Students highly praised Blackboard because it makes reading materials accessible for revision purposes. A student said, "For me, Blackboard is very helpful as it has all the work we have covered uploaded which makes it easy for me to recap the information in preparation for any assessment task." Lecturers are expected to upload all study materials so that students who are registered for that course can easily access it and study in preparation for tests and examinations. This makes Blackboard an indispensable learning platform in the higher education context where students can easily access study material anywhere and anytime.

The use of Blackboard is very essential in the South African context both for undergraduate and postgraduate students. It can be used as a critical resource in case there are campus disruptions, for example the Fees Must Fall protests which resulted in the closure of many universities in South Africa. A student said:

> The use of Blackboard plays a big role especially when university campuses are shut down because of student protests as what happened in 2016. Students do not have to come to campus, but continue learning using Blackboard from their homes.

The use of Blackboard results in the process of teaching and learning continuing regardless of university disruptions that may be happening on campus. All that students need to continue with their learning is the internet and a technological gadget to access learning material on Blackboard in their own time. Such advantages of using Blackboard resulted in one participant summarising the use of the LMS simply as "easy, safer (to use during protests) and efficient."

The use of a Blackboard was also given a standing ovation by PGCE students because it suits their context.

The majority of PGCE students who participated in this research do part-time work and studies at the same time. The use of Blackboard in that context assists them as they do not have to go to campus every day, for example, to submit an assignment. A student said:

> I am working and there are many students in our lectures who are also working. We sometimes come to class late and sometimes we do not come at all because of numerous commitments that include work, illness and family responsibilities. In that context, Blackboard becomes essential as students who are absent from class can easily catch up by going through posted material.

Another student said, "In my view, all PGCE students should be taught using Blackboard because many of them have jobs, and completion of assignments on Blackboard is easier with less interference if protests are to take place." Similarly, another student reiterated that "PGCE students should all be taught using Blackboard as it is interactive and it allows them to work from home or work places." Blackboard allows students to interact among themselves and with the lecturer. It facilitates easy communication among all stakeholders in the teaching and learning process. A student noted that "The use of Blackboard is very conducive as it cuts matters short and it is very easy to communicate."

In spite of the fact that students praised the use of Blackboard in studying the PGCE, they acknowledged that there are critical challenges which hinder their desire for utmost use of the platform. Challenges which were reiterated by all participants are two-fold: poor internet connectivity on campus and lack of funds to purchase internet bundles. A student said:

> It can be very challenging to access Blackboard for assignments and notes especially when you do not have access to internet. Lack of internet connectivity result in students' delay in completing their studies and sometimes with submitting assignments online. Internet connectivity can also be a challenge even when you are on campus where it is supposed to be easier.

Another student who had problems with Blackboard on campus said, "This campus must ensure that they have enough functioning computers with strong internet connectivity for students in order to make the use of Blackboard work." Students would like to maximise the use of Blackboard, but poor internet connectivity and unavailability of enough computers on campus are big hindrances. Some students resort to using their own technology gadgets, but they are also not optimally using Blackboard as they have to buy data bundles since Wi-Fi connectivity is very poor on campus. This resulted in some students not wanting to use Blackboard anymore as was noted by one participant: "It is not a good idea anymore to learn using Blackboard as some of us do not have much access to Wi-Fi or computers on campus or at home." Another student said, "Lecturers should provide free access to the link without using data just for students to access Blackboard."

The challenge of internet connectivity on campus and buying data bundles is resulting in less usage of Blackboard by some students and subsequently leading them to have negative perspectives about the learning platform. A participant said, "I think Blackboard should only be used by lecturers to upload lecture notes and assignments, but the handing in of assignments should be done using hard copies."

Another participant echoed the same sentiment: "Blackboard is fine for lecturers to post notes and assignments, but doing a group task has a lot of difficulties." One student viewed the use of Blackboard as complicated: "Sometimes there are no notes added by the lecturer yet he/she (lecturer) tells you in class that everything is on Blackboard. That makes the whole process (associated with using Blackboard) complicated." Similarly, another participant said, "All PGCE students should be taught using Blackboard, but the challenge is most of the subjects are not listed and no notes are on the platform, but when you come to class the lecturer says all information is loaded on Blackboard.

Despite all the hiccups which students face when using Blackboard, they have said they would like to learn using the platform as it presents a myriad of opportunities which far outweigh its challenges. It helps students with language barriers to go through learning resources over and over until they understand. A student with language barriers said:

> Blackboard is the way to learn today. It helps us students watch posted lectures in digital form over and over again until we understand the content. Some of us grapple with language issues. So, when a lecturer posts his/her recorded lecture to Blackboard, it makes it easy for all students with language barriers to follow. It is an amazing technology which I think must be made compulsory to all lecturers as it is beneficial to students in many ways.

Blackboard is ideal to use as it helps all students regardless of their multilingual and multicultural backgrounds. It is preferred by PGCE students because it allows them to access learning materials anywhere and anytime.

Discussion

The way in which PGCE students are using Blackboard conforms to the CoI laid out by Garrison et al. (2000). Students highly praised the ability to do work anywhere and anytime in their small online groups. This is consistent with the social presence which is the first element in the CoI (Garrison, 2011). Students felt free to create their online communities where they communicate among themselves and also with the lecturer. This resonates with Saudi Arabian students who showered endless praises on the use of Blackboard as it enabled them to share learning material in their different online communities (Hamad, 2017). In the same way, students from Portugal reiterated positive comments about the constructive nature of both social and academic online interactions which they had using Blackboard in their learning activities (Isaias & Issa, 2013). Blackboard offers a variety of learning options which cater for a diverse student population that exists in universities (Kim & Do, 2016). Such diversity promotes student learning which maximises retention in institutions of higher learning.

The cognitive presence manifests on PGCE students in the sense that they used Blackboard to support their work as individuals and in groups. Working as individuals allowed them to make self-discoveries of information and use their thinking skills to solve abstract learning problems. This is consistent with the view of Garrison et al. (2001) on cognitive presence, that it requires students to use their intellectual skills to construct meaning and solve problems. Students are challenged to exercise their reasoning skills when using Blackboard as they will be expected to work out answers to different educational tasks given to them by their lecturers (Hussein, 2016). Students should not make a presumption that Blackboard or any technological device available to them will magically provide answers to their educational tasks. Technology is a tool that needs to be used by humans creatively to solve given problems. It (technology) is useless on its own unless it is used by humans to assist them to achieve their educational goals (Deo, 2016). Thus, in order for an educational goal to be reached, there is a need for students to make use of technology (Blackboard) and most importantly to have an instructor to give guidance.

This brings teacher presence into play. Students cannot learn using Blackboard or any other platform without having a teacher to give directions (Garrison & Arbaugh, 2007). A teacher is irreplaceable in the teaching and learning process (Deo, 2016). As interactive as Blackboard is in students' learning, without a teacher to organise and facilitate those interactions, they come to nothing. A teacher is at the centre of every teaching and learning process as he/she selects relevant materials which students have to study and also assess and offer feedback to students' learning activities (Meda, 2016). Although PGCE students are matured compared to undergraduates, they still depend on a lecturer to guide their entire learning process using Blackboard.

Conclusion

The purpose of this research was to investigate PGCE students' perspectives about learning using Blackboard at a university in South Africa. Students highly regard Blackboard as the most appropriate teaching and learning tool in the 21st century. Although the majority of these students are digital immigrants, they are very enthusiastic about learning using technology, particularly Blackboard, as it allows them to access and upload all learning materials of a subject anywhere and at any time. They praise the learning platform not only because it suits their context (working and studying), but mainly because of its interactive and collaborative nature. Blackboard offers students a wide range of learning options which include studying as individuals or in groups which can be created online and allows them to participate from wherever they are.

It is interesting to note that students' negative comments about Blackboard are not associated with lack of knowledge of using the platform. They mainly emanate from a combination of technical matters such as poor internet connectivity on campus and cost of buying internet bundles. The limited numbers of computers on campus makes students go the extra mile to make it possible to be able to use Blackboard. The learning platform ought to be used with PGCE students as it suits their context of studying while working, promotes student-centred learning which is deeply rooted in the fundamental principles of constructivism, and it is responsive to the 21st century teaching and learning context where Blackboard is now ubiquitous in universities.

References

Arnold, N., & Ducate, L. (2006). Future foreign language teachers' social and cognitive collaboration in an online environment. *Language Learning & Technology,* 10(1), 42–66.

Bertram, C., Mthiyane, N., & Mukeredzi, T. (2013). It will make me a real teacher': Learning experiences of part time PGCE students in South Africa. *International Journal of Educational Development,* 33(2013), 448–456.

Blackboard Company. (2006). *Blackboard Academic Suite brochure.* Retrieved from http://library.blackboard.com/docs/as/bb_academic_suite_brochure_single.pdf

Bodey, K., Ravaga, V., & Sloan, S. (2016). *Exploration of student use of Blackboard Collaborate in fully online courses.* Conference in Adelaide, Australia, Nov 27-30, 2016.

Christie, F., Conlon, T., Gemmell, T., & Long, A. (2004). Effective partnership? Perceptions of PGCE student teacher supervision. *European Journal of Teacher Education,* 27(2), 109-123.

Cohen, L., Manion, L., & Morrisson, K. (2007). *Research Methods in Education.* New York: Routledge.

Council on Higher Education [CHE] (2013). *The Higher Education Qualifications Sub-Framework,* Pretoria: Council on Higher Education.

Creswell, J.W. (2012). *Educational research: Planning, conducting and evaluating quantitative and qualitative research,* Boston: Pearson

Deo, H. (2016). Impact of Interactive Teaching Methodologies on Teaching-Learning Process: A Review. *International Journal of Advanced Research in Education & Technology,* 3(3), 43-48.

Department of Higher Education and Training [DHET]. (2011). *National qualifications framework, Act 67 of 2008. Revised policy on the minimum requirements for teacher education qualifications,* Pretoria: Government Printers.

Department of Higher Education and Training [DHET]. (2015). *National qualifications framework, Act 67 of 2008. Policy on the minimum requirements for teacher education qualifications,* Pretoria: Government Printers.

Ellis, R.K. (2009). *Field Guide to Learning Management Systems,* ASTD Learning Circuits. Retrieved from http://cgit.nutn.edu.tw:8080/cgit/PaperDL/hclin_091027163029.PDF

Ellis, R.A., & Calvo, R.A. (2007). Minimum Indicators to Assure Quality of LMS-supported Blended Learning. *Educational Technology & Society,* 10(2), 60-70.

Fraenkel, J.R., & Wallen, N.E. (2007). *How to Design and Evaluate Research in Education.* Boston: McGraw Hill.

Garrison, R.D. (2011). *E-Learning in the 21st Century: A framework for research and practice.* New York: Routledge.

Garrison, R.D., & Arbaugh, J.B. (2007). Researching the community of inquiry framework: Review, issues, and future directions. *Internet and Higher Education,* 10(2007), 157–172.

Garrison, D.R., Anderson, T., & Archer, W. (2000). Critical inquiry in a text-based environment: Computer conferencing in higher education. *The Internet and Higher Education* 2(2-3), 87–105.

Garrison, D.R., Anderson, T., & Archer, W. (2001). Critical thinking and computer conferencing: A model and tool to assess cognitive presence. *American Journal of Distance Education,* 15(1), 7–23.

Hall, S.L., Scottand, F., & Borsz, M. (2008). A Constructivist Case Study Examining the Leadership Development of Undergraduate Students in Campus Recreational Sports. *Journal of College Student Development,* 49(2), 125-140.

Hamad, M.M. (2017). Pros & Cons of Using Blackboard Collaborate for Blended Learning on Students Learning Outcomes. *Higher Education Studies* 7(2), 7-16.

Hamid, S., Waycott, J., Kurnia, S., & Chang, S. (2015). Understanding students' perception of the benefits of online social networking use for teaching and learning. *The Internet and Higher Education,* 26(2015), 1-9.

Heirdsfield, A., Walker, S., Tambyah, M., & Beutel, D. (2011). Blackboard As An Online Learning Environment: What Do Teacher Education Students And Staff Think? *Australian Journal of Teacher Education,* 36(7), 1-16.

Hussein, E.T. (2016). The Effectiveness of Using Blackboard in Improving the English Listening and Speaking Skills of the

Female Students at the University of Hail. *Advances in Social Sciences Research Journal,* 3(12), 81-93.

Isaias, P., & Issa, T. (2013). E-learning and Sustainability in Higher Education: An International Case Study. *International Journal of Learning in Higher Education,* 20(4), 75-90.

Kim, J., & Do, J. (2016). Learning management system: Medium for Interactive Communication. *International Journal of Applied Engineering Research,* 11(2), 1073-1076.

Kleinveldt, L., Schutte, M., & Stilwell, C. (2016). Embedded librarianship and Blackboard usage to manage knowledge and support blended learning at a South African university of technology. *South African Journal of Library and Information Science,* 82(1), 62-74.

Lansari, A., Tubaishat, A., & Al-Rawi, A. (2010). "Using a learning management system to foster independent learning in an outcome-based university: A gulf perspective." *Issues in Informing Science and Information Technology,* 7(2010), 73-87.

Lapan, D.S., Quartaroli, T.M., & Riemer, J.F. (2012). Introduction to Qualitative Research. In S.D. Lapan, T.M. Quartaroli & F. J. Riemer (Eds.), *Qualitative Research: An introduction to Methods and Designs* (pp. 3-18). San Francisco: Jossey-Bass.

Leeds, E., Campbell, S., Baker, H., Radwan, A., Brawley, D., & Crisp, J. (2013). The impact of student retention strategies: An empirical study. *International Journal of Management in Education,* 7(1), 22-43.

Masi, A., & Winer, L. (2005). A university-wide vision of teaching and learning with information technologies. *Innovations in Education and Teaching International,* 42(2), 147-155.

Meda, L. (2016). Are we helping them to pass or setting them up for failure? Assessment related experiences of partially sighted students. *Journal of Communication,* 7(1), 43-52.

Mohsin, M.A., & Shafeeq, C.P. (2014). EFL teachers' perceptions on blackboard applications. *English Language Teaching,* 7(11), 108-118.

Mukeredzi, T.G., Mthiyane, N., & Bertram, C. (2015). Becoming professionally qualified: The school-based mentoring experiences of part-time PGCE students. *South African Journal of Education,* 35(2), 1-9.

Neuman, L.W. (2011). *Social Research Methods: Qualitative and Quantitative approaches*. Boston: Pearson.

Nomlomo, V., & Sosibo, Z. (2016). From theory to practice: Beginner teachers' experiences of the rigour of the Postgraduate Certificate in Education programme. *Perspectives in Education*, 34(1), 199-215.

Rambe, P. (2017). Spaces for interactive engagement or technology for differential academic participation? Google Groups for collaborative learning at a South African University. *J Comput High Educ*, DOI 10.1007/s12528-017-9141-5

Rambe, P., & Bere, A. (2013). Using mobile instant messaging to leverage learner participation and transform pedagogy at a South African University of Technology, *British Journal of Educational Technology*, 44(4), 544–561.

Pusuluri, S., Mahasneh, A., & Alsayer, B.A.M. (2017). The Application of Blackboard in the English Courses at Al Jouf University: Perceptions of Students. *Theory and Practice in Language Studies*, 7(2), 106-111.

Rahim, H.L., & Chik, R., (2014). Graduate Entrepreneurs Creation: A Case of UniversitiTechnologi MARA, Malaysia. *Australian Journal of Basic and Applied Sciences*, 8(23), 15 20.

Shea, P., Li, C.S., & Pickett, A. (2006). A study of teaching presence and student sense of learning community in fully online and web-enhanced college courses. *The Internet and Higher Education*, 9(3), 175–190.

Szabo, M., & Flesher, K. (2002). CMI Theory and Practice: Historical Roots of Learning Management Systems. *The E-Learn 2002 World Conference on E-Learning in Corporate, Government, Healthcare, & Higher Education*, Canada: Montreal.

Thompson, T.L., & MacDonald, C.J. (2005). Community building, emergent design and expecting the unexpected: Creating a quality eLearning experience *The Internet and Higher Education*, 8(3), 233–249.

Vygotsky, L.S. (1978). *Mind and society: The development of higher psychological processes*, Harvard University Press, MA.

Watson, W.R., & Watson, S.L. (2007). An argument for clarity: what are learning management systems, what are they not, and what should they become? *TechTrends, Springer Verlag,* 51(2), 28-34.

Chapter 6

Student use of technology in Higher Education in Zimbabwe

Silas Parowa Mangwende

Abstract

The purpose of the study was to examine the student use of technology in higher education in Zimbabwe. A case study research design was adopted for this study. A sample of 80 students was taken from two faculties of the Zimbabwe-based Women's University in Africa campus. A questionnaire was used in the case study. The questionnaire was prepared to obtain information on the use of computer and internet by students in a higher education. The data were analysed using percentage distribution tables. It is concluded that students in higher education in Zimbabwe are using the computer for purposes of copying using copy and paste tools whilst preparing assignments and research chapters. The study found that higher education students in Zimbabwe used the internet for both academic and non-academic purposes. Though the internet was utilised for academic purposes it was limited to searching for learning and research material. The study also found that the internet was utilised for sending and receiving emails though the study did not establish the extent to which internet was used for non-academic purposes. It was also established that students minimally use the Websites for learning purposes. Recommendations are suggested to research on the implications of the above conclusions.

Key words: Technology; Students; Higher Education; Curriculum

Introduction and Background

Zimbabwe, a landlocked Southern African country with Mozambique bordering on the east, South Africa on the south, Botswana on the west and twin sister Zambia on the north and north-west, has placed special emphasis on technology. Unleashing the power of technology will lead to various facets of a nation's economic and national development (Shizha & Kariwo, 2011). Thus, Shizha and Kariwo (2011) highlight the importance of technology as a gateway to sustainable economic and national development of any country.

In its endeavour to fully embrace technology, Zimbabwe has embarked on a programme of laying of the fibre optic throughout the length and breadth of the country. Furthermore, the Government of Zimbabwe launched a vigorous introduction of computer education programme in schools, colleges and universities. As a commitment to transform the country into a knowledge-based society by 2020, Zimbabwe has developed a national ICT policy which was adopted in 2005. The policy is aimed at enhancing ICTs in education and one of its objectives is to encourage access to ICTs. The country has partnered with civil society organisations such as the World Links Zimbabwe, African Virtual University, Kubatana Trust of Zimbabwe to mention a few and these have played a significant role towards promoting ICTs in education (Zimbabwe National Policy for ICT, 2014).

The extent to which technology is being integrated into people's everyday lives varies from country to country. Globally, there is an exponential growth in the adoption of technology and in particular internet technology (Ayub, Hamid & Nawawi, 2014). The World Bank (2003) reported a low uptake of technology related programmes in the Zimbabwean tertiary institutions with the proportion of students studying technology related programmes in Zimbabwe's higher institutions of education standing at 24 percent. This is despite the notion that technology related diplomas and degrees are an integral theme for a country's economic and national development.

According to the information and Communication Technology Access by Households and Use by Individuals Survey (2014) report, the proportion of households in Zimbabwe with at least one member of the household with access to internet at home was 33 percent. This suggests that about 4.8 million people out of an estimated population of 14.6 million have access to the internet.

The purpose of internet connectivity is to support and enhance teaching, learning and research activities in higher education institutions. According to Chitanana (2012) internet connectivity enhances the conduct of high calibre research in Zimbabwe tertiary institutions (Chitanana, 2012). Hence, it becomes imperative for students in tertiary institutions to have access to the internet. Chitanana (2012) argued that access to internet plays a significant role for students to participate in a global knowledge society.

Higher institutions of education in Zimbabwe have come under pressure to adopt and implement a number of reforms and policy framework (Zimbabwe National Policy for ICT, 2014). One of the reforms requires higher institutions of education in Zimbabwe to avail internet access infrastructure to students (Chitanana, 2012; Zimbabwe National Policy for ICT, 2014). Thus, moving with trends worldwide all graduates from tertiary institutions in Zimbabwe will demonstrate high level of internet use proficiency.

Over the past years internet connectivity has dramatically become the backbone of teaching and learning processes. To be competitive in the higher education world there is need to have in place sound ICT systems that provide a supportive viable internet environment in which the latter promotes teaching and learning. Thus, there is need for tertiary institutions to embrace the opportunities arising from internet connectivity. Internet connectivity gives students access to unlimited information, beyond the capabilities of traditional libraries (Zimbabwe National Policy for ICT, 2014).

The introduction of e-learning and increased use of e-resources in higher education libraries makes the provision of computers and internet connectivity an imperative development. Linked to the above argument, tertiary institutions in Zimbabwe have invested in ICT systems to enhance the operations of the library. Their library systems are highly digitalised through the installation of Mandarin,

Navision, e-brary and e-granary among other ICT technologies (Zimbabwe National Policy for ICT, 2014). Notwithstanding the fact that internet connectivity will continue to pose a challenge, this will also trigger a major thrust of increasing bandwidths to cater for the anticipated increases in student enrolment, administrative and teaching staff and research publications (Zimbabwe National Policy for ICT, 2014). Hence, it became the thrust of this research to explore how the internet is being used by students in Zimbabwean higher education institutions to support research and learning.

The purpose of the study was to examine student use of technology in higher education in Zimbabwe. The study was guided by the following research objectives:

1. To explore how the computer is being used by students in Zimbabwean higher education institutions.
2. To explore how and where the internet is being used by students in Zimbabwean higher education institutions.

The study has the possibility to contribute to the creation of literature that will benefit ICT policy makers, tertiary institutions ICT departments, stakeholders and technology designers. It will serve as an information base about the inherent uses of technology by students in a higher education environment. Collecting and publishing information about the use of technology by students in a higher education setup can be one strategy to keep ICTs adoption and usage on the public agenda.

Methodology

An interpretive paradigm guided the research in which a qualitative approach was adopted. Subsequently, a case study research design was adopted for this study. Yin (2014) described a case study as an empirical enquiry that investigates a contemporary phenomenon in depth and within its real world context. Thus, the idea of adopting a case study research design was to have a practical enquiry, through the use of data collection methods, on the use of technology by students in higher education in a real university environment. A sample of 80 students was taken from two faculties of the Women's University in Africa. The sample was selected in two stages with the selection of the degree programmes in the first stage and selection of the students in the second stage. At the first sampling stage, eight degree programmes were selected using simple random sampling technique. Twenty degree programmes offered by the university were numbered from 1 to 21 after which random selection took place. At the second sampling stage, ten students were picked from each degree programme using systematic random sampling. The two-stage sampling approach ensured that the sample selected was representative.

A questionnaire was used in the case study. The questionnaire was prepared to obtain information on the use of computer and internet by students in a higher education. The questionnaire consisted of two parts. Part A gathered information on the age of the respondent. To measure the use of the computer and internet by students in a higher education the researcher developed 30 items and these constituted Part B of the questionnaire. The 30 items were adapted from the Zimbabwe National Statistics Agency ICT Household Survey of 2014. The data was analysed using percentage distribution tables.

Results

Table 1: Distribution of students classified by age [N=80]

Age in years	20-24	25-29	30-34	35-39	40-44	45-49	Total
Count	19	15	23	14	6	3	80
Percent	23.8	18.8	28.8	17.5	7.5	3.6	100

Table 1 shows the distribution of the students classified by age. Table 1shows that 42.6 of the respondents were aged 20 to 29 years thus representing the highest student proportion, 46.3 percent were aged 30 to 39 and 11.1 percent were aged 40 to 49 years. Women's University in Africa seeks to address the problem of accessibility of university education to women in Africa (Women's University in

Africa Charter). The majority of the student population is female over the age of 25 years.

Table 2: Distribution of students who used a computer during 2016 classified by type of computer related activity and age

Computer Activity	Age in years						Total
	20-24	25-29	30-34	35-39	40-44	45-49	
Copying or moving a file or folder	13	10	14	11	3	2	53
Using copy or paste tools	10	9	15	9	4	2	49
Sending emails	8	7	14	8	4	3	44
Computing arithmetic formulas	6	7	13	6	3	2	37
Downloading software	5	3	7	4	1	0	20
Creating electronic presentations	10	8	11	7	4	0	40
Creating electronic presentations	10	8	11	7	4	0	40
Students who have used a computer	19	15	23	14	6	3	80

Table 2 shows the number of students who have used the computer to execute various activities.

Table 3 shows percent distribution of students who used a computer within age group during 2016 classified by type of computer related activity and age. The data shows that 66.3 percent of the students used a computer to copy or move a file or folder while 61.3 percent used copy and paste tools on a computer to duplicate or move information. Slight more than half of the students used a computer to send emails. Half of the students used a computer to create electronic presentations.

Students are enticed to use the copy command for creating a duplicate in their assignments due to its easiness to replicate information. Students prepare power point presentations during group presentations and whilst defending research proposals. Thus, students in universities are usually assessed through assignments and research work and hence students in higher education in Zimbabwe are using the computer for purposes of copying, duplicating or moving information using copy and paste tools whilst preparing assignments and research chapters. Students submit soft copies of assignments and research work to the lecturer via emails.

Table 3: Percent distribution of students who used a computer within age group during 2016 classified by type of computer related activity and age

Computer Activity	Age in years					Total
	20-24	25-29	30-34	35-39	40-44	45-49	

Computer Activity	20-24	25-29	30-34	35-39	40-44	45-49	Total
Copying or moving a file or folder	68.4	66.7	60.9	78.6	50.0	66.7	66.3
Using copy or paste tools	52.6	60.0	65.2	64.3	66.7	66.7	61.3
Sending emails	42.1	46.7	60.9	57.1	66.7	100	55.0
Computing arithmetic formulae	31.6	46.7	56.5	42.9	50.0	66.7	46.3
Downloading software	26.3	20.0	30.4	28.6	16.7	0.0	25.0
Creating electronic presentations	52.6	53.3	47.8	50.0	66.7	0.0	50.0
Students who have used a computer	19	15	23	14	6	3	80

Table 4 shows percent distribution of students who used a computer during 2016 classified by type of computer related activity and age. The proportion of students who used a computer for copying or moving a file or folder during 2016 was highest (47.2 percent) for 30-39 age group and lowest (9.4 percent) for 40-49 years age group. The proportion of students who used a computer for duplicating or moving information using copy and paste tools during 2016 was highest (49 percent) for 30-39 age group and lowest (12.2 percent) for 40-49 years age group.

Table 4: Percent Distribution of students who used a computer during 2016 classified by type of computer related activity and age

Computer Activity	Age in years						Total
	20-24	25-29	30-34	35-39	40-44	45-49	
Copying or moving a file or folder	24.5	18.9	26.4	20.8	5.7	3.7	100
Duplicating or moving information using copy or paste tools	20.4	18.4	30.6	18.4	8.2	4.0	100
Sending emails with attachments	18.2	15.9	31.8	18.2	9.1	6.8	100
Computing arithmetic formulas in spreadsheets	16.2	18.9	35.1	16.2	8.1	5.5	100
Downloading software	25.0	15.0	35.0	20.0	5.0	0.0	100
Creating electronic presentations	25.0	20.0	27.5	17.5	10.0	0.0	100
Students who have used a computer	23.8	18.8	28.8	17.5	7.5	3.6	100

The proportion of students who used a computer for sending emails with attached file or document during 2016 was highest (40 percent) for 30-39 age group and lowest (15.9 percent) for 40-49 years age group. The proportion of students who used a computer for computing basic arithmetic formulae in spreadsheets during 2016 was highest (41.3percent) for 30-39 age group and lowest (13.6 percent) for 40-49 years age group. The proportion of students who used a computer for downloading software during 2016 was highest (55 percent) for 30-39 age group and lowest (5 percent) for 40-49 years age group. The proportion of students who used a computer for creating electronic presentations is similar (45 percent) for 20-29 age group and 30-39 years and lowest (10 percent) for 40-49 years age group.

Overall, the proportion of students who used a computer for computer related activities during 2016 was highest among the middle aged students (46. 3 percent) and lowest among the older students (11.1 percent). The data suggests that the older the learner the decrease in the usage of the computer for computer related activities.

The results shows that older students reported lower usage of the computer for copying or moving a file or folder, duplicating or moving information using copy or paste tools, sending emails with attachments, computing arithmetic formulas in spreadsheets, downloading software and creating electronic presentations.

Table 5: Absolute distribution of students who have used the internet classified by type of internet related activity and age

Internet Activity	Age in years						Total
	20-24	25-29	30-34	35-39	40-44	45-49	
Search for learning material	17	13	21	8	3	1	63
Make appointment with lecturer	2	3	1	1	0	0	7
Get information from state department	1	4	3	3	0	0	11
Send or receive emails	8	11	20	13	6	2	60
Participate in social networks	4	10	11	11	4	1	41
Access chat sites	1	5	4	4	3	0	17
Purchase educational material	5	2	3	1	1	1	13
Sell educational material	0	4	3	1	1	1	9
Perform internet banking	0	4	9	2	3	1	19
Do an online course	0	1	4	1	0	1	7
Consult websites for learning purposes	5	7	7	6	2	0	27
Download applications	2	9	6	1	0	0	18
Play or download games, videos or music	2	8	5	2	1	1	19
Read or download e-books	8	10	13	11	4	2	48
Look for a job or attachment	1	2	3	1	0	1	8
Participate in professional networks	0	4	3	2	2	0	11
Send or receive money	3	10	12	7	5	1	38
Students who have used the internet	19	15	23	14	6	3	80

Table 6: Percent distribution of students who have used the internet classified by type of internet related activity and age

Internet Activity	Age in years					Total
	20-24	25-29	30-34	35-39	40-44	45-49	
Search for learning material	89.5	86.7	91.3	57.1	50.0	33.3	78.8
Make appointment with lecturer	10.5	20.0	4.3	7.1	0.0	0.0	8.8
Get information from state department	5.3	26.7	13.0	21.4	0.0	0.0	13.8
Send or receive emails	42.1	73.3	87.0	92.9	100.0	66.7	75.0
Participate in social networks	21.1	66.7	47.8	78.6	66.7	33.3	51.3
Access chat sites	5.3	33.3	17.4	28.6	50.0	0.0	21.3
Purchase educational material	26.3	13.3	13.0	7.1	16.7	33.3	16.3
Sell educational material	0	26.7	13.0	7.1	16.7	33.3	11.3
Perform internet banking	0	26.7	39.0	14.3	50.0	33.3	23.8
Do an online course	0	6.7	17.4	7.1	0.0	33.3	8.8
Consult websites for learning purposes	23.7	46.7	30.4	42.9	33.3	0.0	33.8
Download software and applications	10.5	60.0	26.1	7.1	0.0	0.0	22.5
Play or download games, videos or music	10.5	53.3	21.7	14.3	16.7	33.3	23.8
Read or download e-books	42.1	66.7	56.5	78.6	66.7	66.7	60.0
Look for a job or attachment	5.3	13.3	13.0	7.1	33.3	33.3	10.0
Participate in professional networks	0.0	26.7	13.0	14.3	0.0	0.0	13.8
Send or receive money	15.8	66.7	52.2	50.0	33.3	33.3	47.5
Students who have used the internet	19	15	23	14	6	3	80

Table 6 shows that 78.8 percent of the higher education students have used the internet to search for learning material. The data indicates that approximately 14 percent of the students have used the internet to get information from government department, while about 9 percent have used the internet for making appointment with their lecturers. The data also indicates that about a fifth of the students have used the internet to access chat sites. Meanwhile, slightly more than half of the students have used the internet to participate in social networks.

Table 6 also shows that about 16 percent of the students use the internet to purchase educational material. Within the 20 to 24 years age range the majority (46.7 percent) of the students used the internet to consult websites for learning purposes. Within the 30 to 34 and 40 to 44 years age ranges the majority (39 percent and 50 percent respectively) of the students used the internet to perform internet banking. Of all students aged 25 to 29 years, the majority used the internet to download software and applications. Less than 10 percent of the respondents used the internet to do online courses while about 34 percent used the internet to consult websites for learning purposes. About a quarter of the students used the internet to perform internet banking.

Furthermore, the table shows that within all age groups the majority of the students used the internet to read or download e-books. Overall, sixty percent of the students used the internet to read or download e-books. Almost half of the students have used the internet to send or receive money. Only ten percent of the students have used the internet look for a job or attachment. Table 6 also shows a mere 13.8 percent of the students used the internet to participate in professional networks.

Overall, the data shows few students have used the internet to make appointment with faculty, get information from key government departments and access chat sites for academic and professional guidance. Predominantly, students have used the internet to search for learning material. This suggests that the students mainly use the internet to search for material to complete assignments and research activities. Students are using the internet to search for reading material when preparing for end of semester examinations. The use of the email by 75 percent of the students suggest that students are using emails to send assignments, receive academic material from lecturers and students representatives as well as to share opinions on academic matters. The results also indicate that there is apparently low usage of the internet to get information from government departments. More so, few students are using the internet to create user profiles, post messages to LinkedIn, Xing among other professional networks.

Liquidity challenges in the financial sector might be contributing the low usage of the internet for purchasing educational material. The results suggest that students might have adopted internet banking due to problems in accessing hard cash from the banks. The data also suggest that most students have not adopted online learning due to financial constraints. Shortages of cash bewildering the country and convenience of e-banking might be the factors leading to the use of the internet to send or receive money via Ecocash, textacash, one wallet and other money transfer platforms.

The results indicate that the majority of the respondents used the internet to consult websites for learning purposes though the proportion is low. This suggests that students might not have embraced the idea of consulting websites for learning purposes. Most university libraries in Zimbabwe have inadequate hard copies due stringent budgets. Most of the libraries open doors from 08 00 hours to 16 30 hours during which time the majority of the students are either at work or attending lectures. Most libraries require students to have paid up a certain percentage of tuition fees for the latter to be allowed in the libraries.

Of all students who used the internet search for learning material, 47.6 percent were aged 20 to 29 years, 46 percent were aged 30 to 39 years and 6.4 percent aged 40 to 49 years. Of all students who used the internet for making an appointment with a lecturer 71.4 percent were aged 20-29 years. The proportion of students who used the internet getting information from government departments during 2016 was 45.4 percent for the 20-29 age group and 54.6 percent for the 30-39 age group. The proportion of students who used the internet for sending or receiving emails during 2016 was 55 percent for the 30-39 age group and only 13.4 percent for the 40-49 age group. The proportion of students who used the internet for participating in social networks during 2016 was highest (53.6 percent) for 30-39 age group and lowest (2.4 percent) for 45-49 age groups. This suggests that students also use the internet for non-academic purposes. The proportion of students who used the internet for accessing chat sites during 2016 was highest (47 percent) for the 30 to 39 age group and lowest (5.9 percent) for the 20 to 24 age group.

Table 7: Percent distribution of students who have used the internet during 2016 classified by type of internet related activity and age

Internet Activity	Age in years						Total
	20-24	25-29	30-34	35-39	40-44	45-49	
Search for learning material	27.0	20.6	33.3	12.7	4.8	1.6	100
Make appointment with a lecturer	28.6	42.8	14.3	14.3	0.0	0.0	100
Get information from state department	9.1	36.3	27.3	27.3	0.0	0.0	100
Send or receive emails	13.3	18.3	33.3	21.7	10.0	3.4	100
Participate in social networks	9.8	24.4	26.8	26.8	9.8	2.4	100
Access chat sites	5.9	29.4	23.5	23.5	17.7	0.0	100
Purchase educational material	38.5	15.4	23.0	7.7	7.7	7.7	100
Sell educational material	0.0	44.5	33.3	11.1	11.1	11.1	100
Perform internet banking	0.0	21.1	47.4	10.5	15.8	5.2	100
Do an online course	0.0	12.5	50.0	12.5	0.0	25.0	100
Consult websites for learning purposes	18.5	25.9	25.9	22.2	7.5	0.0	100
Students who used the internet	23.8	18.8	28.8	17.5	7.5	3.6	100

The proportion of higher education students who have used the internet for purchasing or ordering educational material was 53.9 percent for students aged 20 to 29 years compared with 30.7 percent for those aged 30 to 39 years and 15.4 percent for students aged 40 to 49 years. The proportion of higher education students who have used the internet for performing internet banking was highest (57.9

percent) for the 30 to 39 years compared with 21.1 percent that was observed for the 20 to 30 years. The proportion of higher education students who have used the internet for consulting websites for learning purposes was least (7.5 percent) for the 40 to 49 years. Table 9 shows that the proportion of higher education students who have used the internet for studying online was highest (62.5 percent) for the 30 to 39 years.

Overall, table 7 shows that the proportion of students who used the internet during 2016 was highest among the middle aged students (30-39 age group) and lowest among the older students (40-49) age group. The 30 to 39 years old students are employed and have better income than the younger students. The 40 to 49 years students might not have embraced internet banking due to technological challenges. Online learning does not require physical face-to-face learning compared to the traditional classroom learning and due to work commitment this age group prefer online courses. More so, online learning is more expensive and thus attracts the working class who are generally middle aged. Overall, there is no association between the usage of the internet and age of the students. In other words, the internet related activities are independent of student's age.

Table 8: Percent distribution of students who have used the internet during 2016 classified by type of internet related activity and age

Internet Activity	Age in years						Total
	20-24	25-29	30-34	35-39	40-44	45-49	
Play or download games, videos or music.	10.5	42.1	26.3	10.5	5.3	5.3	100
Read or download e-books	16.7	20.8	27.1	22.9	8.3	4.2	100
Look for job or attachment	12.5	25.0	37.5	12.5	0.0	12.5	100
Participate in professional networks	0.0	36.4	27.2	18.2	18.2	0.0	100
Send or receive money	7.9	26.3	31.6	18.4	13.2	2.6	100
Students who used the internet	23.8	18.8	28.8	17.5	7.5	3.6	100

From table 8, of all students who had played or downloaded games, videos or music, 52.6 percent were 20 to 29 years, 36.8 percent were 30 to 39 years and 10.6 percent were 40 to 49. From the table, of all students who read or downloaded e-books, 37.5 percent were 20 to 29 years, half were 30 to 39 years and 12.5 were 40 to 49 years. Table 8 also shows that of all students who looked for a job or attachment, 40 percent were aged 30 to 39 years, a quarter was aged 25 to 29 years and 12.5 percent were aged 40 to 49 years. Of all students who had participated in professional networks, 36.4 percent were 20 to 29 years, 45.4 percent were 30 to 39 years and 18.2 percent were 40 to 49 years.

Table 9: Percent distribution of mostly commonly used internet related activity

Internet Activity	Total
Search for learning material	78.8
Send or receive emails	75.0
Read or download e-books	60.0
Participate in social networks	51.3
Send or receive money	47.5
Consult websites for learning purposes	33.8
Students who have used the internet	80

Table 9 shows that students have mostly used the internet to search for learning material, send or receive emails and read or download e-resources.

Only 5.3 of the respondents within the 20 to 24 years age group used the internet at the work. This suggests that a minority of this age group are employed. Thus, students within the 20 to 24 years age group rely on the university internet for both academic and non-academic purposes. Table 10 shows that students within the older age groups used the work place internet more frequently compared to usage at the university. This suggests the internet connectivity might be faster and efficient at the work place.

Table 10: Distribution of students who have used the internet at various locations in 2016

Used Internet at	Age in years												Total	
	20-24		25-29		30-34		35-39		40-44		45-49			
Home	6	31.6	8	53.3	14	60.9	4	28.6	6	100	3	100	41	51.3
Workplace	1	5.3	7	46.7	15	65.2	7	50.0	6	100	3	100	39	48.8
University	19	100	9	60.0	10	43.5	7	50.0	1	16.7	1	33	47	58.8
Another person's home	0	0.0	3	20.0	2	8.7	1	7.1	0	0.0	0	0.0	6	7.5
Another person's workplace	0	0.0	2	13.3	1	4.3	0	0.0	0	0.0	0	0.0	3	3.8
Free community internet facility	0	0.0	1	6.7	1	4.3	1	7.1	0	0.0	0	0.0	3	3.8
Paid community internet facility	5	26.3	1	15.0	1	4.3	1	7.1	1	16.7	0	0.0	9	11.3
Number of students	19	23.8	15	18.8	23	28.8	14	17.5	6	7.5	3	3.8	80	100

Overall, 51.3 percent of the respondents used the internet at home, 48.8 percent at the work place and only 11.3 at a paid internet café. The majority of the students (58.8 percent) used the internet at the university. The results indicate that the points of accessing internet related activities by higher education students have mostly been through universities laboratories or libraries followed by home-based broadband and thirdly the workplace. This suggests that students opt for cheaper access to internet-based information.

Table 11: Percent distribution of students who have used the internet at various locations during 2016

Used Internet at	Age in years						Total
	20-24	25-29	30-34	35-39	40-44	45-49	
Home	14.6	19.5	34.1	9.8	14.6	7.4	100
Workplace	2.4	17.9	38.5	17.9	15.4	7.9	100
University	40.4	19.1	21.3	15.0	2.1	2.1	100
Another person's home	0.0	50.0	33.3	16.7	0.0	0.0	100
Another person's workplace	0.0	66.7	33.3	0.0	0.0	0.0	100
Free community internet facility	0.0	33.3	33.3	33.3	0.0	0.0	100
Paid community internet facility	55.6	11.1	11.1	11.1	11.1	0.0	100
Students who used the internet	23.8	18.8	28.8	17.5	7.5	3.6	100

From table 11, of all students who had used the internet at home, 34.1 percent were 20 to 29 years, 43.9 percent were 30 to 39 years and 22 percent were 40 to 49 years. From the table, of all students who had used the internet at the workplace, 20.3 percent were 20 to 29 years, 56.4 percent were 30 to 39 years and 23.3 percent were 40 to 49 years. Of all the students who had used the internet at university, 59.5 percent were 20 to 29 years, 36.3 percent were 30 to 39 years and 4.2 percent were 40 to 49 years. Of all the students who had used the internet at another person's workplace, two-thirds were 20 to 29 years. Of all the students who had used the internet at a paid community internet access facility, 66.7 percent were 20 to 29 years.

Discussion

In this study, the researcher examined student use of technology in higher education in Zimbabwe. The researcher started with an exploration on how the computer is being used by students in Zimbabwean higher education institutions. The researcher then proceeded with another exploration on how and where the internet is being used by students in the higher education institutions.

The results show that the most frequently used computer functions are copying, moving or duplicating information. It a common practice that students in universities are usually assessed through assignments and research work and hence students in higher education in Zimbabwe are using the computer for purposes of copying, duplicating or moving information using copy and paste tools whilst preparing assignments and research chapters. Additionally, students Zimbabwean higher education institutions use a computer to create electronic presentations. The findings are comparable with those of Tsvere, Nyaruwata and Swamy (2013) who revealed that students use a computer to prepare presentations such as power point presentations. Similarly, Rahman (2011) whose study examined the use of computers among students at a college in Saudi Arabia reported that the computer was mainly used to create power point presentations.

The results indicate that students have frequently used a computer to send emails. It is now becoming a common practice that students in Zimbabwean tertiary institutions submit soft copies of assignments and research work to the lecturer via emails. These findings are comparable with those of Arthur and Brafi (2011) who revealed that students have adopted internet technology to communicate and network among themselves. The results are also consistent with Jones (2012) who observed that most college students frequently use electronic mail to communicate with lecturers and fellow students. This suggests that students use the convenience of email to submit assignments and research chapters any time of the day and from any place. In their study on access and use of the internet by undergraduate students in Ugandan universities, Ndawula (2011) established that sending and receiving emails is a widely practiced internet related activity among university students.

The results also concurs with Castan-Munoz, Duart and Sancho-Vinuesa (2014) who found that internet use in higher education comprised of communicating with lecturers and other students and online chats on academic issues. This suggests that the email is a very significant tool to submit assignments and supervised projects-in-progress and distribute course outlines and soft copies of learning materials. Using the internet to send or receive emails enables one to one, one to many and many to one interaction. However, the findings are inconsistent with Amenyedzi, Lartey and Dzomeku (2011) who found medium to low usage of email and browsing by the students.

The proportion of students who used a computer for computer related activities was highest among the middle aged students and lowest among the older students. Older students reported lower usage of the computer for copying or moving a file or folder, duplicating or moving information using copy or paste tools, sending emails with attachments, computing arithmetic formulas in spreadsheets, downloading software and creating electronic presentations. In a study which analysed the determinants of the digital and computer penetration, Chinn and fairly (2004) revealed that the use of a computer for computer related activities depend on the individual's exposure to the functions of a computer.

As further argued by Chinn and fairly (2004), lower levels of computer related activities are attributed by the extent of computer navigational skills. According to the researchers a higher percentage of young people is associated with a greater rate of computer usage, while a lower computer usage rate is a common feature among the older generations. Similarly, Tsvere et al (2013) asserted that age explains the different patterns in the usage of the internet among the university students. Thus, there is an association between computer activity and age of the student.

The results show that students frequently use the internet to search for learning material. The results are supporting Castano-Munoz et al, (2014) who found that internet use in higher education was focused on searching information, looking up for course lines and other course materials. In their study on internet usage by university students and academics, Tsvere et al, (2013) revealed that students most frequently use the internet for learning purposes, research and as an information source. The researchers added that the internet is used to find information for preparing assignment material. Similarly, Bhatti (2010 established that the internet is frequently used for research related work. In this study it appears students used the internet to carry out research projects and dissertations. In their study on how the internet is used by students in tertiary institutions in Sunyani Municipality, Arthur and Brafi (2011) established that higher education students use the internet technology to search for information for assignments.

This suggests that the shortened time taken by students to write and submit assignments and research projects might be the motivation for using the internet. Yet in another study, Jones (2012) noted that the internet is a significant tool for searching information to do research and assignments. This suggests that a greater proportion of students tend to prefer information found on Google and search engines as well as web sites as assignment material. The findings are also consistent with those of Kumar and Manjunath (2013) who found that students use the internet in support of their learning. Ndawula (2011) found that the internet is used as a source of information in locating references for the review of literature when writing assignments and research projects. Ndawula (2011) established that the use of the internet has become significant in accessing E-notes to beef up traditional lecture notes.

The internet is a source of vast loads of information used for research work by students (Chitanana, 2012). In the study of the internet in face-to-face higher education, Castano-Munoz et al, (2014) found that internet use in higher education was frequently used for looking up for course learning material. Contrary to this study's findings, Amenyedzi Lartey and Dzomeku (2011) reported low usage of the computer and internet for research and learning. The researchers also found medium to low usage of email and browsing by the students.

The internet has become a commonly used platform for communicating with faculty and fellow students. Castano-Munoz et al, (2014) in their study on the internet in face-to-face higher education revealed that students use the internet to communicate with lecturers and fellow students and engage in online discussions on academic issues. More so, Rahman (2011) observed that most tertiary institutions around the globe have mandatorily adopted communication through email between faculty and students. Few students are using the internet to access chat sites for academic and professional guidance.

The results also indicate that there is apparently low usage of the internet to get information from government departments. This suggests there is low interaction between higher education students and key government departments such as the Zimbabwe Council for Higher Education (ZIMCHE), Zimbabwe Manpower Development Fund, Medical Research Council of Zimbabwe and Research Council of Zimbabwe.

The results show that there is low usage of the internet to purchase educational material. This suggests students might not be augmenting lecture notes. This is despite the fact that the internet is a paramount technology in facilitating online courses. Ndawula (2011) observed that students access web sites for online educational materials.

Findings from this study show that the uptake of students in consulting websites for learning purposes is low. The results are showing that the middle-aged higher education students are the majority in the use of the internet to consult websites for learning. Hence, the proportion of students making use of the internet to consult websites for learning purposes is low. This suggests that lecturers are not putting lectures and learning material on the web to encourage more face-to-face contacts with students.

The results show that most of the students in Zimbabwean tertiary institutions are using the internet to read or download e-books. These findings are supporting Bhati (2010) who examined internet usage in the changing higher education environment at the Islamia University of Bahawalpur and found that university students make use of the internet to download books and journal articles for assignment information material. Similarly, Chitanana (2012) argued that students access electronic journals and e-books on the internet. In their study about awareness and usage of electronic information resources among postgraduate students in Nigeria, Akpojotor (2016) revealed that traditional books, journals and magazines have transformed into e-books, e-journals and e-magazines and thus the physical library has turned digital. Thus, the advantage of these electronic resources is that they are easily read or downloaded from any location.

Another advantage was cited by Chitanana (2012) who asserted that most universities provide access to the e-resources through computer laboratories, computer centres, libraries and campus wide wireless networks. More so, Rahman (2011) observed that most tertiary institutions around the globe have formulated policies that make it mandatory for students to use the internet as an academic information source and channel. Such developments prompt reading or downloading from the internet.

Another interesting revelation from this study is that there is no association between the usage of the internet for playing or downloading games, videos or music, reading or downloading e-books, looking for a job or attachment, participating in professional networks and sending or receiving money and age of the students. In other words, the internet related activities are independent of student's age.

The results indicate that few students are using the internet to create user profiles, post messages to LinkedIn, Xing among other professional networks. These findings are comparable with those of Tsvere et al, (2013) who found that the internet is less frequently used by students as a platform to share academic knowledge using blogs. Similar findings were observed in Kim's (2011) study on the effects of internet use on academic performance among South Koreans students when the researcher reported low usage of internet related activities such as blogging, internet surfing and shopping attributed by inadequate digital skills.

Students have mostly used the internet to search for learning material, send or receive emails and read or download e-resources. Therefore, developments in ICTs have enabled the internet to serve as a platform for academic research and learning material. These results are comparable to those of Ayub et al, (2014) who established that the internet was being used to address students' academic concerns. Similarly, Ndawula (2011) found that students in higher education institutions use the internet for academic based usage namely as a learning and research tool, source for e-notes and references and distance learning.

The results also show that students are using the internet for non-academic purposes as evidenced by half of the students who have used the internet to participate in social networks. Ayub et al, (2014) found that exchanging ideas and knowledge via email and socializing via social networks such as LinkedIn, twitter and Facebook has changed the worldview on internet from merely an academic platform to a non-academic one. Ndawula (2011) further revealed the use of the internet for non-academic purposes namely downloading games and music though this usage was reported to be minimal.

The results indicate that the points of accessing internet related activities by higher education students have mostly been through universities laboratories or libraries followed by home-based broadband and thirdly the workplace. Tsvere et al, (2013) revealed that access to the internet by students is mostly in or through university library. However, the researchers observed that students use the internet for internet related activities at the workplace more than they do at home. This means understanding per capita income, investment in communication infrastructure and expenditure on internet is very critical. In their study, Chinn and Fairlie (2004) suggested that the level of income, availability of communication infrastructure and costs of internet are to a large extent the determinants of place of accessibility to the internet. Internet usage at home might be limited by household expenditure on ICT equipment.

Zimbabwe National Statistics Agency ICT Household Survey (2014) revealed that internet charges a share of 6.4 percent of total household ICT expenditure on services. Internet connectivity in university might be enhanced by strong investment in telecommunication infrastructure. Besides universities boasting of a strong investment in telecommunication infrastructure, Chitanana (2012) argued the use of the internet at university was high since students have access to electronic journals, e-learning and emails free of charge. Researchers Schmidt and Cohen (2013) argued that accessibility is a major contributing factor in the use of the internet.

Contrary to the results of this study, Arthur and Brafi (2011) observed that students have mostly accessed the internet through internet cafes more than they do through university libraries and computer laboratories. Thus, in their research it was revealed that students reported high usage of internet related activities through internet cafes. Similarly, in his study on the use of computers among students of dental college in Saudi Arabia, Rahman (2011) found that most of the students used the internet at home.

Conclusion

It is concluded that students in higher education in Zimbabwe are using the computer for purposes of copying, duplicating or moving information using copy and paste tools whilst preparing assignments and research chapters. The study found that higher education students in Zimbabwe used the internet for both academic and non-academic purposes. Though the internet was utilised for academic purposes it was limited to searching for learning and research material. The study also found that the internet was utilised for sending and receiving emails though the study did not establish the extent to which internet was used for non-academic purposes. It was also established that students minimally use the websites for learning purposes.

References

Akpojotor, L.O. (2016). Awareness and usage of electronic information resources among postgraduate students of library and information science in Southern Nigeria. *Library Philosophy and Practice* (e-journal).

Amenyedzi, F.W.K, Lartey, M.N., & Dzomeku, B.M. (2011). The use of computers and internet as supplementary source of educational material: A Case study of the senior high schools in the Tema Metropolis in Ghana. *Contemporary Educational Technology*, 2(2), 151-162.

Ayub, H., & Nawawi, P. (2014). Use of the internet for academic purposes among students in Malaysian Institutions of Higher Education. *The Turkish Online Journal of Educational Technology*, 13(1).

Bhatti, R. (2010). Internet use among faculty members in the changing higher education environment at the Islamia University of Bahawalpur, Pakistan. *Library Philosophy and Practice, 1-9.*

Chinn, M.D., & Fairlie, R.W. (2004). *The Determinants of the global digital divide: A cross-country analysis of computer and internet penetration.* Economic Growth Center. Yale University. Discussion paper.

Chitanana, L. (2012). Bandwidth management in universities in Zimbabwe: Towards a responsible user base through effective policy implementation. *International Journal of Education and Development Using Information and Communication Technology* 8(2), 62-78.

Jones, S. (2012). *The internet goes to college: How students are living in the future with today's technology.* Pew Internet and American Life Project.

Kim, S. (2011). *Effects of internet use on academic achievement and behavioural adjustment among South Korean adolescents:* Mediating and moderating roles of parental factors. Child and Family Studies Dissertations Paper 62.

Kumar, B.T., & Manjunath, G. (2013). Internet use and its impact on the academic performance of university teachers and researchers: A comparative study. *Higher Education, Skills and Work-based Learning.* 3(3).

Ndawula, S. (2011). *Access and use of the internet: A case of undergraduate students in public universities of Uganda.* 3rd seminar 16th of June 2011.

Rahman, G. (2011). Use of computers among students of dental college in Saudi Arabia. *J Educ Ethics Dent.* 1, 12-17.

Schmidt, E., & Cohen, J. (2013). *The New digital age: Reshaping the future of people, nations and business.* John Murray: London.

Tsvere, M., Nyaruwata, T.L., & Swamy, M. (2013). Internet usage by university academics: Implications for the 21st century teaching and learning. *International journal of science and research* 2(9).

Zimbabwe National Policy for ICT. (2014).

Zimbabwe National Statistics Agency. (2014). *Information and Communication Technology household survey. Access by households and use by individuals' report.*

Chapter 7

Teaching pre-service teachers to integrate technology for inclusive classrooms with deaf learners in Tanzania

Bernadatte Namirembe

Abstract

In recent years there has been increasing interest in the integration of technology in teaching and learning. The growing diversity of learners in the classrooms has increased the need to train teachers to use technology integrated pedagogy. Training teachers to use technology in instruction in many developing countries is challenging because of beliefs, computer proficiency, teacher characteristics and other factors. Direct Instruction (DI) is recommended in such situations to provide pre-service teachers with a step-by-step training. Feedback can play a vital role in this context to find out the effectiveness of the instruction approach. The study was therefore conducted to assess pre-service teachers' perception of Direct Instruction approach in teaching TCVIS course, which aimed at training pre-service teacher to integrate technology in teaching in order to meet the needs of diverse learners including the deaf. In this cross-sectional study with both quantitative and qualitative approaches, all the Bachelor of Education with Special Needs - Hearing Impairment (BEDNS-HI) undergraduate students who were currently studying in the second year and third year were included in this study. A self-administered questionnaire and focus group discussions served as study tools. The questionnaires were handed out to 63 pre-service teachers. The questionnaires consisted of 25 items and each item scored on a five-point Likert scale. Results of the study show that most pre-service teachers had a positive perception of DI approach of teaching because they were able to pragmatically learn. There were however differences in perception in relation to age, gender and computer proficiency. The study provides an insight on how teachers in developing countries can be trained to integrate technology in pedagogy.

Keywords: Technology, Direct Instruction; Technology integrated pedagogy; Inclusive classrooms

Introduction and Background

Technology has facilitated paradigm shifts in education and transformed the way students learn. Advances in technology have motivated educators to develop and implement new and innovative strategies to teach students for more effective and meaningful learning (Chai, Koh & Tsai, 2010). But the direct impact of technology on effective and meaningful learning and the use of technology by teachers in the teaching has remained minimal in many developing countries. This lack of impact may be attributed to the barriers to the integration of technology for learning in higher education which include technology infrastructure, faculty effort, technology satisfaction, and graduates' competency (Teo & Zhou, 2014; Kihoza, Zlotnikova, Bada, & Kalegele, 2016). It is also attributed to challenges for both learner and learning environments in which technology is not omnipresent via laptops, tablets, smartphones, etc., technology skills are rarely important. This study defined technology according to Luppicini (2005) in two forms; technology as a tool and technology as a process. Technology (process) means the construction uses and the organization of knowledge for the achievement of practical purposes in intellectual and social contexts. Technology (tool): material construction and operation of physical systems based on systematic knowledge of how to design artefacts. Educational Technology: is the field concerned with the design, development, utilization, management, and evaluation of processes and resources for learning.

With the growing reliance on technology to transform teaching and learning, many developed countries are providing pre-service teachers with skills on technology. Strong pre-service education on the use of ICT is said to be important because it can help to counter the possibilities of transmission-oriented school practices in the assimilation of beginning teachers (Chai et al., 2010). There are however many problems in preparing student teachers in developing countries for ICT integration. Many student teachers, for example in Tanzania do not have enough, while some do not have any exposure to use of ICT and therefore lack the basic ICT skills. According to United Republic of Tanzania [URT], 2007), education should integrate ICTs in pre-primary, primary, secondary and teacher education.

Conversely, though the government of Tanzania supports the use of technology, the current syllabi focuses on teaching ICT as a subject and less on using ICT as a pedagogical tool (Kihoza et al., 2016). While universities and other tertiary institutions in Tanzania have made a significant investment in ICT, ICT facilities in the education system are mainly used for ICT skills training and very few universities are making use of digital learning environments. It appears imperative for teacher educators to design technology integrated courses where technology content development for teaching is part of the curriculum.

A technological content visualization and instruction skills (TCVIS) course was developed for the Bachelor of Education with Special Needs (BEDSN) program at Archbishop Mihayo University College of Tabora (AMUCTA) in Tanzania. The course aimed at providing pre-service teachers or student teachers with basic skills to integrate technology in instruction through content visualisation using direct instruction (DI). This study addresses how the teachers were trained and the pre-service teachers' perceptions toward the quality of instruction. Quality of instruction includes aspects such as didactic characteristics of instruction, task adaptation, and classroom climate, relationships with peers and relationships with teachers (Hermans, Klerk, Wauters, & Knoors, 2014). This study focused on the exploring the student teachers' perception of the approach of instruction used in the training.

Diverse learners and teaching

In the era of inclusive education, teachers meet many challenges in classes with diverse learners who include deaf learners with different mode of communication. How the teacher can accommodate these differences has now become a major concern of teacher trainers. According to (Hattie, 2012) in the past many schools resorted to structural methods such as streaming the students according to their capabilities, but despite that, classes remain full of heterogeneity which is a disadvantage in the teaching and learning process for the learner. Conversely, often teachers lack suitable teaching materials.

This makes it difficult to deliver feasible and sound knowledge to diverse learners especially the deaf who seemingly are the most challenging learners in inclusive classrooms (Mayer, 2016). According to Knoors and Marschark (2014) the educational needs of deaf students are specific and need extra attention. For instance deaf learners lag behind hearing peers in language development. Therefore, it is important to expect seeing cognitive divergences between deaf and hearing learners. Deaf children are far more variable than hearing children. Additionally, their background provides deaf children with more learning challenges than the hearing children.

Teaching the whole class is unlikely to make the lesson clear for all learners due to diversity.in most classrooms. The teacher must use the skill of identifying the similarities and differences across students. Differentiation relates mainly with structuring the classes so that all the students are working from where they start, to allow maximal opportunities to attain success conditions of the lessons (Hattie 2012). How the teacher can accommodate these differences is the major concern. Research shows that learners, especially struggling learners need to combine different input modalities to learn effectively (Knoors & Marschark, 2014; Sergers & Verhoven, 2014; Hibbing & Rankin-Erickson 2003).

According to Hibbing and Rankin-Erickson (2003) different forms of visualisation such as films provide time contexts, setting details and important situational information for those learners who have less prior knowledge of the subject being addressed especially the deaf. Pictures also are supreme in their capacity to arouse emotions while text illustrations serve an affective-motivational function to learners. A study by Sergers and Verhoeven (2014) on deaf learners' opportunities of multimedia learning, shows that the deaf learners can benefit from a combination of written text, sign language and visual pictures in the long run.

Hibbing and Rankin-Erickson (2003) gave an elaborate explanation on the importance of different input modalities in instruction practice. Pictures make reading a text more enjoyable, results in positive attitudes towards reading and influence the time readers are willing to spend on the text, which is beneficial to learners. Stiller (2007) explains further that the modality principle recommends using spoken rather than written texts in conjunction with pictures, because learners learn more effectively in computer-based and book-based environments when spoken rather than visual texts are used concurrently with dynamic or static pictures.

Additionally, Schmidt-Weigand and Scheiter (2008), showed that the visualizations in this material increase learning success compared to a text-only format. Ginns (2005) reviewed research on the modality effect, the educational practice of presenting to-be-learned graphical information visually, and related textual information through an auditory mode. Meta-analytic methods were applied to 43 independent effects (39 between-subjects designs, 4 within-subjects designs). Major hypotheses regarding the instructional benefits of presenting information across modalities were supported.

The teachers need to provide students with essential elements necessary to achieve the learning intentions. Kihoza, et al., (2016) and Koh and Divaharan (2011) affirm that the education system contemporary time for inclusive classes, require student teachers to be imparted with competencies and skills to integrate information and communication technology (ICT) into their future teaching and learning practice. Wang and Chen (2006) however observe that some level of proficiency in technological skills is needed for teachers to integrate technology effectively. It is essential to note that many teachers in developing countries such as Tanzania find a challenge in preparing sound materials for teaching especially the visualisation materials because of time and lack of financial support. Providing student teachers with basic technological skills that make them to be familiar with the current versions of ICTs, specifically knowledge on how to develop multimedia presentations for teaching could be of great importance to the teaching and learning process. Student teachers can learn to use ICT to prepare, store and reuse these materials with minimal alterations depending on the feedback from class. They can also learn how they can prepare and use the materials to support learners especially the deaf who normally exhibit less prior knowledge.

Technology integration in the classroom

Literature identifies three broad categories of how teachers use technology in schools (Braak, Tondeur & Valcke, 2004; Inan & Lowther, 2009); technology for instructional preparation, technology for instructional delivery, and technology as a learning tool. The focus of the teacher education course studied in this paper is teacher professional use of technology for instructional preparation, particularly preparing instructional materials and technology for instructional delivery particularly organising the text and visual materials to create power point presentations. Therefore, teachers can present a lesson by means of a projector or students may use the materials to self-teach on a computer or tablet or phone.

On the other hand, Robinson (2003) and Braak, et al., (2004) identified factors which directly and indirectly effects teachers' technology integration in teaching which included age and teachers' computer proficiency. From literature it is also deduced that new graduates have more knowledge on technology integration and feel better prepared compared to more experienced peers because teachers who recently graduated from a teacher preparation program would be more technology competent (Jones & Madden, 2002; Hicks, 2011) and more prepared to integrate technology into classroom instruction (Ertmer & Ottenbreit-Leftwich, 2014).

Experienced teachers may have less computer proficiency and confidence to integrate technology; thus limiting opportunities for changing their daily teaching practices or trying new technologies in their classrooms. According to Hicks (2011) there is also a strong relationship between the frequency of computer use and the number of computers available in the classroom. However, studies continuously indicate that computer access is necessary but not sufficient for establishing technology integration in the classrooms (Christensen, 2002; Smeets, 2005). It is not surprising to see limited technology integration even when computers and necessary software are available in the classroom (Lowther, Inan, Daniel Strahl, & Ross, 2008; Cuban, Kirkpatrick, & Peck, 2001). Another factor raised in literature is that technology integration is influenced by the support that comes from peers, administration, and the community (Hernandez-Ramos, 2005; Lumpe & Chambers, 2001; Hicks, 2011) Nonetheless, teachers' computer proficiency is found to be one of the most important factors affecting their technology integration.

A study by Christensen (2002) revealed that the climate under which teachers' practice may alter teacher beliefs as well as their classroom practices. Furthermore, Hicks (2011) and Inan and Lowther (2009) provided a comprehensive list of contextual factors such as resources, administrative support, parental support, technical support, and professional development that impacted teachers' beliefs. Teachers' computer proficiency was another variable found to influence teachers' beliefs in United States. Teachers like to feel comfortable with technology before using technology (Ottenbreit-Leftwicha, Glazewskib, Newbyc, & Ertmerc, 2010; Ertmer & Ottenbreit-Leftwich, 2014).

The teacher demographic characteristics, which impact teacher computer proficiency and readiness, were not found to influence the teachers' beliefs. This finding suggests that there might be other teacher-level variables that influence teacher beliefs such as subject area of teaching and previous technology training (Hew & Brush 2007; Lih-Juan, Jon-Chao, Jeou-Shyan, Shih-Hui, & Hui-Chuan, 2006) The study concluded that the major factors having the most important influence on technology integration was the teachers' readiness to integrate technology, after controlling for other model variables. Ertmer and Ottenbreit-Leftwicha (2014) concur that teachers who feel ready and confident to integrate technology used technology more frequently in their classroom instruction.

A study by Kayombo and Mlyakado (2016) assessed the status of secondary school teachers' knowledge and skills necessary for the implementation of the Information and Communications Technologies (ICTs) policy for basic education in Tanzania. In particular, the study examined Tanga Municipality and Mwanza region secondary school teachers' ability to use computers (the basic ICT tool) for the professional practices; and solicited teachers' opinions on the integration of ICT in secondary education. Self-administered questionnaires with closed-ended and open-ended questions were used to gather data from the respondents.

The sample consisted of 26 schools; 11 schools drawn from Tanga Municipality and 15 drawn from Mwanza region. From 26 surveyed schools, a total of 124 respondents were recruited, both males and females. The study found several gaps which exist between the ICT policy and the real practice or implementation of ICT objectives in education such as limited teachers' awareness and training in ICT integration, and electricity and ICT facilities supply in most schools. The study therefore recommended that the education sector, in Tanzania, should strive to work shoulder to shoulder with other sectors in the country for the improvement of education in general and integration of ICT in teaching and learning processes.

Similarly, Ndibalema (2014) carried out a study on teachers' attitudes towards the use of ICT as a pedagogical tool in secondary schools in Tanzania. The aim of the study was to provide a better understanding of ICT as a pedagogical tool. The development of this study was influenced by various concerns of educational stakeholders about the level of teachers' competence on the use of ICT as a pedagogical tool. The data collection tools involved questionnaire and interview. A total of 80 teachers, through random sampling in 10 schools were involved in this study at the first phase of data collection and 10 teachers were obtained through purposive sampling from 2 schools at the second phase. It was found that teachers have positive attitudes towards the use of ICT as a pedagogical tool but they did not integrate it in their teaching effectively. Also, low familiarity with ICT use as a pedagogical tool among teachers was found to be a problem. The study concluded that the use of ICT as a pedagogical tool in Tanzania seems to be a critical situation among teachers.

Students' perceptions of instructional approaches

Student teachers who have acquired higher level of technological skills are more willing to use technology in the classroom since they possess a strong sense of self efficacy with computer use (Chai et al., 2010). Though some level of proficiency in technological skills is needed for teachers to integrate technology effectively (Wang and Chen, 2006), but the pedagogical use of ICT for specific subject matter to be taught (Chai et al., 2010) is also vital. Deciding on how to instruct teachers to integrate ICT in pedagogy depends much of their prior technological skills. Zheng and Young (2006) compared two types of instruction: Problem–based Learner-centred Learning Cycles (PBLC) and Direct Instruction (DI), both of which reflected research findings concerning best instructional practices. Analysis of Logistic Regression identified a model that differentiated the PBLC and DI approaches in areas of pre-service teachers' perceived knowledge of technology integration and technology competencies, and revealed that pre-service teachers reporting more favourable computer use and more knowledge of portfolio development are more likely to be in the PBLC approach.

A study by Gasaymeh, AlJa'afreh, Al-Dmour and Abu Alrub, (2016), investigated university students' preferences of the principles of constructivism in their learning of programming languages through the use of information and communication technologies (ICTs). Factors which influence these preferences were investigated too. The respondents for this study were 193 students from three courses teaching programming languages in computer labs. A cross-sectional survey design was used. The study involved one group of students who were taught programming languages based on the principles of constructivism and another group which was taught using the lecture-based teaching methods. The results showed that the higher education students preferred the use principles of constructivism in learning language programming using ITCs. It is important to note that all the students involved in the study had basic computer skills. This study was carried out in one of the universities in Jordan. . In another study by Greene, Costa, Robertson, Pan, and

Deekens (2010) observed that prior knowledge and self-beliefs had an influence on the use of self-regulated learning processes.

Cognitive or physical skills are the foundation on which more advance learning is built. Before students can develop creativity in various things they need basic skills and information. The difference between novices and experts is that experts have mastered the skills to the point when they can perform them with precision (Arends, 2009). For the purpose of novice teaching, direct instruction (DI) model is appropriate in order to train each skill step-by-step (Table 1.). The DI is designed to promote masterly of skills and knowledge that can be taught step-by-step. It requires careful orchestration by the teacher, it is task oriented and keeps the student actively engaged (Arends, 2009). Accordingly, TCVIS course training adopted the Engelmann's (1980) model since it involved training several skills in sequence. Additionally, the student teachers needed to gain proficiency in ICT and to integrate ICT in their pedagogical skills.

Problem Statement

In order to improve student learning and to meet the needs of diverse learners, some educators have recommended the integration of ICT in teaching. Unfortunately, increased availability of technology in the schools does not necessarily lead to improvement in classroom teaching practices (Lim & Chai 2008; Lowther et al., 2008). Likewise, there is insufficient empirical support to claim that access to technology has either increased test scores or improved the quality of instruction to enhance student learning (Lowther et al., 2008; Cox & Marshall, 2007). Research suggests that these disappointing outcomes are frequently associated with teachers lacking the necessary skills to integrate technology into the classroom (Kayombo & Mlyakado, 2016; Ndibalema, 2014; Eteokleous, 2008; Braak, et al., 2001). A survey in Tanzania has indicated that the biggest percentage of teachers felt not prepared to integrate technology in their instruction (Kayombo & Mlyakado, 2016; Ndibalema, 2014). Technology integration research has identified several critical variables thought to be important in regard to achieving effective technology integration.

These include teacher characteristics (i.e. age and gender), teacher's mode of instruction, access to technology and proficiency, support, belief and so on. Teachers' computer proficiency is found to be one of the most important factors affecting their technology integration (Inan & Lowther, 2009). Based on the factors that influence effective technology integration, it is pertinent to find teachers' perceptions of the training given to integrate technology in teaching. The views of students normally prove that they possess sharp observation skills and provide valuable and applicable information.

Theoretical Framework

The theoretical framework drawn in this study is based on two models. The Direct Instruction (DI) model and the TPACK mode. These two models are chosen because TPACK emphasize teachers making connections between their Technological, Pedagogical, and Content Knowledge when integrating technology (Chai et al., 2010), while DI emphases progressing step by step at the pace of a learner (Arends, 2009). The study adopted the DI instructional model according to Magliaro, Lockee and Burton (2005) and Engelmann's (1980) which helps the facilitator to follow every student through given steps in Table 1 below.

The DI model draws its theoretical support from behavioural theories and social learning theory. Behavioural theories of learning also endorse the use of DI. Behavioural theories maintain that humans learn to act in certain ways in response to positive and negative consequences. Of particular importance is Skinner's work on operant conditioning and his ideas that humans learn and act in specific ways as a result of how particular behaviours are encouraged through reinforcement. Teaching according to behavioural principles concurs with the DI principles. It involves clear statement of objectives that describe with precision the behaviours they want students to learn, provide learning experiences such as practice in which students' learning can be monitored and feedback provided. It emphasizes rewards to particular behaviour exhibited (Arends, 2009).

Similarly, the social learning theory according to Albert Bandura posits that much of human learning comes through observation of others. According to Bandura (1986) there are three steps in observation learning. First, the learner has to pay attention to the stimuli or behaviour learned. Second, the learner has to retain and remember the behaviour and third, the learner must be able to reproduce the learned behaviour. Conducting a DI lesson also follows the same steps and principles.

Table 1. Engelmann's Direct Instruction model, adopted from Magliaro, Lockee, and Burton (2005, p. 46)

STEP	ACTIVITIES
Introduction	1. Introduction of new concept based on previously mastered skills knowledge
Main Presentation	2. Presentation: Fast-paced, scripted explanation, demonstration designed to elicit only one concept. The target concept must be reinforced with appropriate examples and non-examples.
Practice	3. Students are provided with opportunities to verbally respond either through a set of questions or practice tasks, in order to indicate their learning of the concept and their ability to connect it to further examples.
	4. Feedback: Teacher either confirms correct student response or provides corrections and repetition of the missed items.
	5. Independent practice: After group work, students engage in self- directed practice in workbooks. Teacher monitors progress and provides guidance when needed.

The theoretical and empirical work of Vygotsky (1978) also identified two critical elements of DI as essential to learning from a social perspective. Vygotsky used the concept of scaffolding and his paradigm of the zone of proximal development (ZPD) to represent the teaching as an assisted performance model. For Vygotsky (1978), scaffolding refers to the instructional support provided to students as they learn new skills, content, and dispositions. Information is broken down into manageable, smaller amounts of recognizable knowledge; skills are broken down to subskills to ensure a sequential, step-by-step acquisition of the target objectives aided by teacher guidance, questioning, hints, and so forth. Essential in this process is a task analysis that thoroughly examines what is to be learned, and the trajectory of the development of knowledge to meet that objective.

The ZPD is, according to Vygotsky (1978), the "distance between the actual developmental level is determined by individual problem solving and the level of potential development is determined through problem solving under adult guidance or in collaboration with more capable peers" (p. 86). From a DI perspective, teachers are striving to meet each student within the zone by a clear analysis of the task, constant assessment of understanding and provision of support when and as needed, and practice first with the teacher, then with peers, then independently.

Therefore, DI continues to hold potential as an effective teaching method, particularly in technology mediated learning environments. Computer based programs have been designed to model instructor-led DI approaches while leveraging the technological ability to provide feedback, remediation, and guided practice, all essential components of the DI process and all of which contribute to its effectiveness (Magliaro et al., 2005). Therefore, the mode of instruction depends more on the students' characteristic. In this case, where many student teachers hardly had any knowledge on basic ICT skills, DI may be the most appropriate approach of teaching.

The study also used TPACK framework. TPACK was derived from three key knowledge sources i.e. technological knowledge (TK), pedagogical knowledge (PK) and content knowledge (CK) and it is a framework used in incorporating ICT design projects to help teachers develop connections between TK, PK, and CK. (Mishra & Koehler, 2006; Chai et al., 2010). According to Mishra and Koehler (2006), content, pedagogy and technology are central for developing good teaching. Basing on TPACK the TCVIS course was designed. TPACK framework was used to guide the development a course and identification of constructs needed to integrate ICT into classroom within the context of what is possible in Tanzania secondary schools and the relationship between the constructs.

Unlike TPACK, TCVIS involves providing student teachers with basic skills of ICT and ICT integration in teaching in inclusive classrooms. Hence, in addition to TPACK's key knowledge sources: technological knowledge (TK), pedagogical knowledge (PK) and content knowledge (CK) (Mishra & Koehler, 2006) the course designers added other constructs for the purpose of providing skills to meet the needs of diverse learners. Additionally, emphasis was on skills not knowledge. The course (TCVIS) was therefore conceptualised as a seven-construct framework as the diverse kinds of skills student teachers have to learn to integrate technology and meet the need of diverse learners especially the deaf as shown in Figure 1. It comprises four main skills sources:

1. Technological Skills (TS) – skills of technology tools.
2. Content Skills (CS) – knowledge of subject matter.
3. Visualization Skills (VS) – skills of how to visualise concepts.
4. Instruction Skills (IS) – skills of planning presentation for teaching.

It also comprises of nine other types of technology integration skills that are derived through the connections among technological skills, content skills, visualisation skills and instructional skills. These are:

5. Technological Content Skills (TCS)—skills of subject matter representation with technology.
6. Technological Instruction Skills (TIS)—skills of teaching using technology.
7. Content Visualisation Skills (CVS) – skills of visualising subject content.
8. Visualization Instruction Skills (VIS) – skills of teaching with visualization.
9. Technological Content Instructional Skills (TCIS) – skills of teaching subject content with technology.
10. Technological Content Visualization Skills (TCVS) – skills of visualizing subject matter content with technology.
11. Technological Visualisation Instruction Skills (TVIS) – skills of teaching visualization with technology.

12. Content Visualization Instruction Skills (CVIS) – skills of teaching subject content with visualization.

13. Technological Content Visualization Instruction Skills (TCVIS) – Skills of teaching subject content within visualization using technology.

The thirteen constructs demonstrate the diverse kinds of skills student teachers had to learn in the TCVIKS course in order to be able to integrate technology into teaching to meet the needs of diverse learners including the deaf.

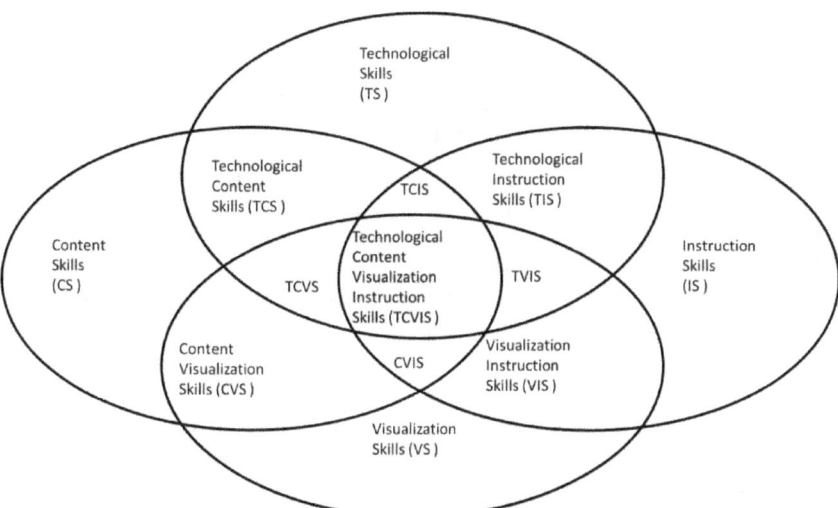

Figure 1. TCVIS framework, a revised TPACK framework (Mishra and Koehler, 2006, p.1025).

Table 2. TCVIS constructs and skills taught

TCVIS constructs	Skills taught
Technological skills (TS)	- Foundation knowledge to use of computers - Using office applications (specifically word processors, PowerPoint.) - Creating multimedia presentation using PowerPoint. - Accessing and downloading online resources (particularly pictures and videos) - Searching visualizations for specific subject content. - Making presentations using computers and LCD projectors. - Making short video from the surrounding, role plays and dramas using cameras and smartphones and how to store them on computers - Using a mind mapping programme. - Designing activities that integrate technology. - Storing non technological visuals by using technology
Content skills (CS)	- Identifying subject key words, abstract and difficult words for visualisation using a 3 tier model. - Making a subject abstract concepts concrete through visualization
Visualization skills (VS)	- Using Internet visualisation resources. - Developing subject specific visuals - Using cameras and smart phones office to create and store visuals from the surrounding. - Developing mind maps with visuals - Adding visuals in PowerPoint presentations - Storing non technology visual resources - Making video clips from drama.

Instruction skills (IS)	- Combining text, video, pictures and non-technology resources in power point presentations - Preparing and organising presentations using information technology that enhances students learning for a lesson. - Supporting learning activities in different teaching settings using technology. - Using visualisations for instruction.

Steps of TCVIS teaching

Figure 2 TCVIS instruction model

TCVIS instruction model combines DI approach to teaching with TPACK framework of technology training. The juxtaposition is thought to be the best approach to develop vital skills of student teachers in order to integrate technology in teaching. TCVIS training followed four steps. In each step a new skill was introduced and was trained following the five steps of DI. In Each subsequent step focus was also on the integration of the new skill with skill(s) already learnt. Using DI instruction principle of guided practice, student teachers carried out activities that strengthened the connections among their technological skills, content skills, visualization skills and instructional skills. The facilitators provided contextualized feedback with positive and encouraging statements. The student teachers' proficiency of all TCVIS was developed through projects that required them to develop and present PowerPoint presentations on different topics from the secondary school syllabus.

Purpose of the study

The purpose of this study was to assess the student teachers' perceptions towards the instruction approach used to integrate technology in teaching (TCVIS). Furthermore, this study was designed to investigate differences in perceptions of student teachers based on their characteristics (i.e. age, gender and computer proficiency).

Significance of study

This study investigated pre-service teachers' perceptions of the model of instruction used in teaching the TCVIS course. The deaf learners are emphasized in this study because the researcher believes that they are the most challenging learners to many teachers due to hearing loss and therefore, ability to meets their needs implies meeting the needs of all learners. Consequently, the course focused on how the teacher meets the needs of the deaf learners, which automatically implies meeting the needs of all learners. One of the major factors that influence learning and performance in school is the teachers' instructional strategies. The most effective strategies are those where learning is visible to both the teacher and the learners (Hattie, 2014).

It also imperative to note that the way student teachers are taught is normally the way they will teach their future learners. Since this is always the case, it is of importance that student teachers duplicate teaching strategies that positively influence learning. This requires careful modelling of teaching strategies that have been proven useful especially for diverse and struggling learners. Importantly, the modelled teaching strategies should have made learning visible to the learners. It is pertinent therefore to explore learners' perceptions of the quality of instruction of the TCVIS course. How they viewed the quality instruction is important for future instruction in classrooms with diverse learners.

The increased use of ICT in enhancing, learning of deaf learners made it vital to include ICT in the curriculum for student teachers. Since many pre-service teachers have little or no exposure to technological skills and pedagogical skills using ICT, it was very important to seek their views on the quality of instruction. Student teachers' perceptions of the quality of instruction are very vital because they have to develop a strong level of self-efficacy to be able to use ICT in the teaching and learning process. This information will be used to inform the pre-service teacher trainers and the course developers of the best practices and the challenges future course review and course improvement. The pre-service teachers also need to learn how the use of technology simplifies the preparation of visualization materials in particular and all teaching materials in general. They also need to reflect on the teaching model and how it made learning visible to them for better future replication. The information will also be invaluable in designing subsequent research as well as provide a baseline with which to compare the future research findings and make sound inferences.

Research questions

This study was guided by the following research questions:

1. What are student teachers' perceptions of the use of DI approach in teaching the TCVIS course?

2. How different are the student teachers' perceptions in relation to age, gender and computer proficiency?

Methodology

A cross sectional survey was conducted to find out the student teachers' perceptions towards the use of the DI in teaching TCVIS course. The study included 63 student teachers, 29 of these were year three and 34 were in year two. All student teachers currently in their second year and third year for the programme of Bachelor of Education with Special Needs-Hearing impairment (BEDSN-HI) in this private university in Tanzania were involved in the study because they were the only classes that were taught this course. For the purpose of this study, a questionnaire was developed and self-administered to assess students' perceptions of the quality of instruction received. Questionnaires were chosen because the study employed a survey design, the target group was an adult educated population and for time saving.

The study used open ended questionnaires because they are easy to administer and analyse. They also provided greater precision to respondents. The questionnaire consisted of 47 items divided into five scales. For each statement, student teachers had to indicate to what extent they agreed with the statement (1 = strongly disagree; 2 = Disagree; 3 3 Neutral; 4 = Agree; 5 = Strongly Agree). Focus group discussions were also conducted with student teachers to verify the information from survey questionnaires and examine the differences in student teachers' perceptions basing on age, gender and computer proficiency. The researcher asked student teachers for permission to involve them in the study and assured them anonymity.

Data Analysis

Questionnaires were analysed using descriptive statistics that included means and standard deviations that were used to answer the first research question regarding student teachers' perceptions of the use of the DI model in teaching the course. The purpose of using descriptive statistics was to provide summary of the data in order for easy description. T-tests were used to examine the differences between participants' perceptions in the use of the DI model based on the groups of participants. Focus group discussions were used to examine the difference between participants based on their gender, age and the extent of their computer proficiency. Data from focus group discussions was analysed using a phenomenological approach. The discussions were recorded and coded and the most similar views were selected.

Results

Table 4 shows the students' means and standard deviations on the five scales of the questionnaire that measured student teachers' perceptions in the use of the DI approach in teaching the TCVIS course.

Student teachers' perception of DI approach

A total of 63 student teachers filled the survey questionnaires. Most student teachers had positive perceptions toward the DI approach of instruction (M = 4.67 and 4.33, SD = 0.47 and 0.75). The comparison between the two groups (the third year class and second year) also suggested no significant difference in the student teachers' perceptions (p < .05 t = 3.33). (See table 4). Specifically, examining at each step of the DI approach, student teachers across both groups recorded a strong opinion towards instruction and facilitation (M = 28.27 and 33.27, SD = 0.62 and 0.75). The perception of the two groups was also compared using a t test. The results suggested no significant differences in student teachers perceptions of both groups on how the faculty instructed and facilitated (p < .05 t = 5.21).

Both groups also recorded positive perceptions towards guided practice (M = 4.29 and 4.41, SD =0.45 and 0.73 as shown in table 4. The comparison between the two groups also suggested no significant difference in the student teachers' perception of how the faculty provided guided practice (p < .05 t = 4.90). In addition, both groups recorded positive perceptions on feedback (M = 4.43 and 4.33, SD = 0.47 and 0.75). The comparison between the two groups also suggested no significant difference in the student teachers' perceptions to the feedback provide (p < .05 t = 1.74).

Both groups had positive views on independent practice (M = 4.44 and 4.33, SD = 0.60 and 0.75). The comparison between the two groups also suggested no significant difference in the student teachers' perceptions to independent practice (p < .05 t = 4.18).

Difference in perceptions.

Focus group discussions were used to capture the difference in perception according to student teachers' characteristics and computer proficiency. 54% of the student teachers had no or poor computer proficiency (table 3). Student teachers with low computer proficiency reported that the faculty clearly stated the objectives of every activity and demonstrated every step of using technology in the course. Student teachers particularly who had no and poor computer proficiency reported that they had no difficulty in grasping the skills because they were broken down into small manageable skills and presented step by step.

One student said that, "I have learned what l thought was very difficult. She explains and demonstrates everything step-by-step, handled small bits at a time and that made it easy for someone like me without background knowledge of technology to follow." While another one said that, "My lack of computer skills made me very slow and l found myself lagging behind the whole class. However, the lecturer supported me until l was able to move with the whole group."

However, some student teachers with no or poor computer proficiency reported that inadequate skills of using computers slowed them down and suggested the need for more practice to master and to be confident to use technology in teaching. The difference in perceptions was registered in the level of confidence. Those who had less ability or no ability of using computer expressed less confidence.

On the other hand, results from the 46% of student teachers with moderate to very good computer proficiency showed that student teachers treasured the faculty's support in activities to have increased their learning opportunities which showed their positive perception towards the DI instruction. One student remarked that, "Everything seemed easy as she demonstrated it, but when we were given chance to practise, l always got stuck but she was always ready to demonstrate again and again until l could do it on my own".

Student teachers' positive perceptions were also shown by their expression on how they benefited from feedback provided by faculty. They reported that it helped them to improve skills and to correct misconceptions. It also increased motivation. One student remarked that,

On many occasions we assumed we were doing the right thing only to be informed by the lecturer of some step we did not consider. This was very common when selecting the kind of visuals to use. For example, we developed short films for abstract concepts but feedback on each individual film enabled me to become creative and finally developed the competence of visualizing abstract concepts concretely using technology.

There was a difference in perceptions due to age and gender registered. Most of the female student teachers had low perception of the DI approach showed by the limited confidence they expressed in many aspects of the course. However, most of the male student teachers showed readiness to integrate technology in instruction, which showed their positive perception of the DI approach of instruction. Male student teachers reported that they had benefited from independent practice through the project given by the faculty member. They reported that it helped them to improve skills and develop confidence. It also increased motivation. One student remarked that,

The project helped me to master and become creative. I am confident l can now use technology to prepare and teach my subject." I have learnt how to download pictures and films, how to create short films from the surrounding, how to store materials for future use. In fact, l have learnt a lot of things that l can use confidently when teaching.

Eight percent of the student teachers were above 30 years and 92% below 30 years. Results from focus group discussions showed that student teachers below and above 30 years had high perception of the DI approach. They reported that the method helped them to learn new pedagogy different from the conventional. One student remarked, "From what l have learnt in this course, my lessons will be so interesting, interactive and use technology."

The student teachers above 30 years reported that the course enabled them to acquire more knowledge and creativity. They also found the course very challenging but interesting and enjoyable. They reported a positive perception of the DI approach because of the step-by-step approach and the guided and independent practice that enable them to acquire considerable computer proficiency.

Table 3. Shows characteristics of respondent

1st Group	N	%	2nd Group	N	%	Total (%Total)
Age			**Age**			
19 and younger	3	10	19 and younger	2	6	5 (8)
20 – 24 years	13	45	20 – 24 years	19	56	32 (51)
25 – 29 years	12	41	25 – 29 years	9	26	21 (33)
30 and older	1	4	30 and older	4	12	5 (8)
Gender			**Gender**			
Female	7	24	Female	15	44	22 (35)
Male	22	76	Male	19	56	41 (65)
Previous computer proficiency	9		**Previous computer proficiency**	9	26	18 (29)
No ability	8	31	No ability	8	24	16 (25)
Poor	6	27	Poor	13	38	19 (30)
Moderate	6	21	Moderate	4	12	10 (16)
Good	0	21	Good	0	0	0 (0)
Very good		0	Very good			

Table 4. Shows descriptive analysis, t test and comparisons of perceptions (1st group and 2nd group)

Scale	Group	N	M (SD)	t test
Instruction and facilitation	1st	29	4.35 (0.62)	5.21
	2nd	34	4.27 (0.75)	
Guided practice	1st	29	4.29 (0.45)	4.90
	2nd	34	4.41 (0.73)	

Feedback	1st	29	4.33 (0.47)	1.74
	2nd	34	4.43 (0.75)	
Independent practice	1st	29	4.44 (0.60)	4.18
	2nd	34	4.33 (0.75)	
General perception	1st	29	4.67 (0.47)	3.33
	2nd	34	4.33 (0.75)	

Discussion

The study was aimed at investigating student teachers' perceptions of the quality of the direct instruction (DI) approach used in teaching of the Technology Content Visualization and Instruction Skills (TCVIS) course. Based on the findings from questionnaire surveys and focus group discussions, the student teachers of both groups involved in the study had positive perceptions on the DI approach of teaching which involved step-by-step instruction, guided practice, feedback and independent practice. The results reveal that the student teacher had a positive perception of each step of direct instruction used, which accrued to the general perception. This finding concurs with the remark of Arends (2009) that for the purpose of novice teaching, DI model is appropriate in order to train each skill step-by-step. The results also reveal that those with low and no computer proficiency reported that they found it easy to follow the step-by-step instruction to the extent that they were able to do what they earlier on perceived very difficult.

The study also confirms the earlier study by Zheng and Young (2006) which compared two types of instruction: Problem–based Learner-centred Learning Cycles (PBLC) and Direct Instruction (DI). The study identified that what differentiated the PBLC and DI approaches was the pre-service teachers' perceived knowledge of technology integration and technology competencies. Young's study revealed that pre-service teachers with more knowledge of computer use and more knowledge of portfolio development preferred the PBLC approach. Most of the participant in this study had poor to moderate computer proficiency that is why they highly perceived the model because they were able to benefit from a step-by-step.

Additionally, the earlier observation by Gasaymeh et al. (2016), that the higher education students preferred the use principles of constructivism in learning language programming using ITCs also supports the current. The student in Gasaymeh et al. (2016) study had basic computer skills. However, most of the students in the current study were virgins, this was the first time they touched a computer. It is important to note that the instruction started from teaching basic computer skills including switching on and switching of the computer. This implies that the perception and preference vary from context to context depending on the prior knowledge of the participants involved.

The findings also showed that there was a difference in student-teachers' perceptions in relation to gender, age and computer proficiency. The student teachers with moderate to high computer proficiency had more positive perception than those with low and no computer proficiency. The fact of the matter is that, although these students thought they had good and moderate proficiency, they were not actually at a level of the students Gasaymeh, et al. (2016) used in the study who preferred to use the principles of constructivism. The students in the current study reported that they often got stuck while they thought the procedure was very easy. Therefore, they were grateful for the DI step of guided practice because it offered an opportunity to update their knowledge base. Greene et al. (2010) observed that prior knowledge and self-beliefs had an influence on the use of self-regulated learning processes.

This finding also sheds more light on different steps of DI instruction in teaching and why they contributed to the overall student teachers' positive perception on the method. Martin (2006) elaborated that setting goals improves enjoyment of learning, participation in class and persistence. Therefore, the clear statement of goals for each activity might have led to the positive student teachers perception of DI since self-fulfilment would depend on achieving the well-known set goals. Hattie (2014) supports that teachers and students need to know the learning intentions and need to move from a single idea to multiple ideas, and to relate and then extend these ideas such that learners construct and reconstruct knowledge and ideas. It is learner's construction of this knowledge and ideas that is critical. Hattie also adds a key insight that focusing on learning through the eyes of students, appreciating their fits and starts in learning and their often non-linear progressions to the goals, supporting their deliberate practice, providing feedback about their errors and misdirection, and caring that the students get the goals and that students and teacher's passion for the material being taught are ingredients to learning.

Feedback is another step of indirect instruction that student teachers applauded as it assisted them to improve their skills and clear misconceptions. Hattie (2012) explained that feedback is most powerful when the nature of feedback is related to the student's degree of proficiency. He highlighted the notion of progress feedback which is expressed in relation to the expected standard, to prior performance or to success or failure on a specific part of the task. He therefore suggested that it is important to provide formative feedback relative to the criteria of success rather than comparative to whether other students are. Indeed in the current study, using DI model, the student teachers were able to get progressive feedback on each skill and step. This also explains why they positively perceived the model of DI. Chan (2006) concurs that feedback was more likely to enhance self-efficacy when it was formative rather than summative, self-referenced rather than comparative referenced.

The current study also confirms Bandura's (1986) social learning theory, which is one of the theoretical foundation of the DI model. Bandura explained that learning follows three steps including, paying attention to the stimuli or behaviour learned, retaining and remembering the behaviour and reproducing the learned behaviour. Therefore, in the current study student teachers perceived highly the step of independent practice which provided them with the opportunity to reproduce the learned behaviour, therefore confirmed that they had understood. The findings are also in agreement with the findings of 35 eminent researchers who summarized that the major empirically grounded processes for learning relate to multiple ways of knowing, multiple ways of interacting, multiple opportunities for practice and much feedback to know that we are learning (Magliaro, Lockee & Burton, 2005). Hattie (2012) observed that learning is not always pleasurable and easy, it requires overlearning at certain point and spiralling up and down the knowledge continuum. Students appreciate that learning is not always pleasurable and easy and indeed can engage with and enjoy the challenge that learning entails.

The major limitations to the study was that the instruments used to collect data were not validated. Since the instruments were developed by the researcher and were not piloted anywhere, then they pose a challenge of validity. Secondly, the population involved in this study was small only involving two groups of students. More studies need to be carried out on the subsequent groups of students who will do this course. Therefore, the results of this study cannot be generalized to represent the whole country. Further research is needed to dwell into this model and find out its effectiveness in teaching ICT integration in pedagogy.

Conclusion

This study provides insight into how to train teachers in the integration of technology in in the Tanzanian context. The results are encouraging, because most students reported to have benefited and enjoyed the TCVIS course. The findings suggest that the DI model can be used to train pre-service teachers to use technology in teaching if they have poor computer background. All pre-service teachers, no matter their background in technology and age, were able to appreciate the instruction model. Conversely, there is an advantage of integration of technology in pedagogy that the current study has highlighted that is important to note: it increases teachers' innovativeness and creativity. The teachers can meet the needs of diverse learners, especially the deaf, if they are reflective, creative and innovative. ICT integration into pedagogy is capable of enhancing those skills. Although that can only be possible if teachers gain computer proficiency. To gain computer proficiency, teachers must have continuous access to technology devices such as computers. Hence, it is time for schools to have technological resources for teaching. Similarly, teachers' colleges and universities should consider including such a course in the curriculum for teachers. All pre-service teachers need knowledge and skills to integrate technology into instruction because the 21st century classes are full of diverse learners.

References

Arends, I. R. (2009). Learning *to teach* (8th ed.). Boston: McGraw Hill Higher Education

Bandura, A. (1986). *Social foundations of thought and action.* Englewood Cliffs: Prentice Hall.

Braak V. J., Tondeur, T., & Valcke, M. (2004). Explaining different types of computer use among primary school teacher. *European Journal of Psychology of Education, 19*(4) 407-422.

Chai, C. S., Koh, J. H. L., & Tsai, C.C. (2010). Facilitating pre-service teachers' development of technological, pedagogical, and content knowledge (TPACK). *Educational Technology & Society, 13*(4), 63-73.

Chan, C. Y. J. (2006). *The effect of different evaluative feedback on student's self-efficacy in learning,* PhD Thesis, Faculty of Education, University of Hong Kong.

Chen, C. H. (2008). Why do teachers not practice what they believe regarding technology integration? *Journal of Educational Research, 102*(1), 65-75.

Christensen, R. (2002). Effects of technology integration education on the attitudes of teachers and students. *Journal of Research on technology in Education, 34*(4), 411-433.

Cox, M., & Marshall, G. (2007). Effects of ICT: Do we know what we should know? *Education and Information Technologies, 12*(2), 59-70.

Cuban, L., Kirkpatrick, H., & Peck, C. (2001). High access and low use of technologies in high school classrooms: Explaining an apparent paradox. *American Educational Research Journal, 38*(4), 813-834.

Ertmer A. P., & Ottenbreit-Leftwich, T.A. (2014). Teacher technology change: how knowledge, confidence, beliefs, and culture intersect. *Journal of Research and Technology in Education, 42*(3), 255-284.

Eteokleous, N. (2008). Evaluating computer technology integration in a centralized school system. *Computers & Education, 51*(2), 669-686.

Gasaymeh, A.M, AlJa'afreh, A.I, Al-Dmour, A & Abu Alrub, M. (2016). 'Higher education students' preferences for applying the principles of constructivism in learning programming languages with the use of ICT. *Journal of Studies in Education, 6*(3), 168-187.

Ghan, M. (2011). *'The effects of prompts and explicit coaching on peer feedback quality'* (Doctoral dissertation). University of Auckland.

Ginns, P. (2005). Meta-analysis of the modality effect. *Learning and Instruction, 15*(4), 313-331.

Greene, J.F., Costa, L, Robertson, J, Pan, Y., & Deekens, V. M. (2010). 'Exploring relations among college students' prior knowledge, implicit theories of intelligence, and self-regulated learning in a hypermedia environment'. *Computers & Education,* 55, 1027-1043.

Happel, K. I., Zheng, M., Young, E., Quinton, L. J., Lockhart, E., Ramsay, A. J., & Nelson, S. (2003). Cutting edge: Roles of toll-like receptor 4 and IL-23 in IL-17 expression in response to klebsiella pneumoniae infection. *The Journal of Immunology, 170*(9), 4432-4436.

Hattie, J. (2012). *Visible learning for teachers: Maximizing impact on learning.* New York: Routledge.

Hermans, D., Klerk, A. Wauters, L & Knoors, H. (2014). Quality of instruction in bilingual schools for deaf children. In Marschark, M., Tang, G., & Knoors, H., (Eds.), *Perspectives on deafness: Bilingualism and bilingual deaf education* (pp. 272-293). New York, Oxford University Press.

Hernandez-Ramos, P. (2005). If not here, where? Understanding teachers' use of technology in Silicon Valley schools. *Journal of Research on Technology in Education, 38*(1), 39-64.

Hew, K. F., & Brush, T. (2007). Integrating technology into K-12 teaching and learning: Current knowledge gaps and recommendations for future research. *Educational technology research and development, 55*(3), 223-252.

Hibbing, A.N. & Rankin-Erickson, J.L. (2003). A picture is worth a thousand words: using visual images to improve comprehension. *The Reading Teacher, 56*(8), 758-770.

Hicks, S. D. (2011). Technology in today's classroom: Are you a tech-savvy teacher? The Clearing House. *Journal of Educational Strategies, Issues and Ideas, 84*(5), 188-191.

Hightower, A. M. (2009). Tracking US trends: States earn B average for policies supporting educational technology use. *Education Week: Technology Counts, 28*(6), 30-33.

Inan, F. A., & Lowther, D. L. (2010). Factors affecting technology integration in K-12 classrooms: A path model. *Educational Technology Research and Development, 58*(2), 137-154.

Jones, S., & Madden, M. (2002). *The Internet goes to college: How students are living in the future with today's technology.* Washington, DC: Pew Internet & American Life Project.

Kayombo, J. J. & Mlyakado, B. P. (2016). 'The Paradox of ICT integration in secondary education in Tanzania: Assessment of teachers' ICT knowledge and skills in Tanga and Mwanza regions. *International Journal of Research Studies in Educational Technology, 5*(1), 17-27.

Kihoza, P., Zlotnikova, I., Bada, J., & Kalegele, K. (2016). Classroom ICT integration in Tanzania: Opportunities and challenges from the perspectives of TPACK and SAMR models. *International Journal of Education and Development using Information and Communication Technology, 12*(1), 107-128

Knoors, H., & Marschark, M. (eds.), (2014). *Teaching deaf learners: Psychological and developmental foundation,* New York: Oxford University Press.

Koh, J. H. L, & Divaharan, S. (2011). Instructional model developing pre-service teachers' technology integration expertise through the TPACK-developing. *Educational Computing Research, 44*(1) 35-58.

Lih-Juan, C., Jon-Chao, H., Jeou-Shyan H. and Shih-Hui, C., & Hui-Chuan, C. (2006). Factors influencing technology integration in teaching: A Taiwanese Perspective. *Innovations in Education and Teaching International ProQuest Education Journals, 43*(1), 57-68.

Lim, C. P., & Chai, C. S. (2008). Teachers' pedagogical beliefs and their planning and conduct of computer-mediated classroom lessons'. *British Journal of Educational Technology, 39*(5), 807-828.

Lowther, D. L., Inan, F. A., Daniel Strahl, J., & Ross, S. M. (2008). Does technology integration "work" when key barriers are removed? *Educational Media International, 45*(3), 195-213.

Lumpe, A. T., & Chambers, E., (2001). Assessing teachers' context beliefs about technology use. *Journal of Research on Technology in Education, 34*(1), 93-107.

Luppicini, R. (2005). A systems definition of educational technology in society. *Educational Technology & Society, 8* (3), 103-109.

Magliaro, S. G., Lockee, B. B., & Burton, J. K. (2005). Direct instruction revisited: A key model for instructional technology. *Educational technology research and development, 53*(4), 41-55.

Mayer, C. (2016). Addressing diversity in teaching deaf learners to write. In Marschark, M., Lampropoulou, V., and Skordilis, E.K., (Eds.). *Perspectives on deafness: Diversity in deaf education* (pp. 271-298). New York: Oxford University Press.

Mishra, P., & Koehler, M. J. (2006). Technological pedagogical content knowledge: A framework for teacher knowledge. *Teachers College Record, 108*(6), 1017-1054.

Ndibalema, P. (2014). Teachers' attitudes towards the use of Information Communication Technology (ICT) as a pedagogical tool in secondary schools in Tanzania: The case of Kondoa district. *International Journal of Education and Research, 2*(2), 1-16.

Ottenbreit-Leftwicha, T.A., Glazewskib, K.D, Newbyc, T.J., & Ertmerc, E. P. (2010). Teacher value beliefs associated with using technology: Addressing professional and student needs. *Journal of Research and Technology in Education, 55*(3), 1321-1335.

Robinson, W. I. (2003). *External, and internal factors which predict teachers' computer usage in K-12 classrooms.* Detroit: MI, Wayne State University.

Schmidt-Weigand, F., Kohnert, A., & Glowalla, U. (2010). A closer look at split visual attention. In system-and self-paced instruction in multimedia learning. *Learning and Instruction, 20*(2), 100-110.

Segers, E. & Verhoeven, L. (2014). Benefits of technology for deaf and hard-of-hearing students. In Knoors and Marschark (Eds.). *Educating deaf learners: Creating a global evidence base* (pp. 481-501). New York: Oxford University Press.

Smeets, E. (2005). Does ICT contribute to powerful learning environments in primary education? *Computers & Education, 44*(3), 343-355.

Stepp-Greany, P. (2002). Student Perceptions on Language Learning in a Technological Environment: implications for the new millennium. *Journal of Language Learning & Technology, 6*(1), 165-180.

Stiller, K. D. (2007). The modality principle in multimedia learning. An Open Question: When Speech Fails to Foster Learning? *Open Innovation "Neue Perspektiven im Kontext von Information und Wissen"*, 129-144.

Teo, T. & Zhou, M. (2014) 'Explaining the Intention to Use Technology among University Students: A Structural Equation Modelling Approach'. *Journal of computing in higher education: Research and integration of instructional technology, 26* (2), 124-142.

United Republic of Tanzania (2007). Information and Communication Technology (ICT) policy for basic education, Dar es Salaam, Ministry of Education and Vocational Training (MoEVT). Retrieved from http://moe.go.tz/pdf/ict%20policy%20for%20basic%20education.pdf

Vygotsky, L. S. (1978). *Mind and society: The development of higher psychological processes* (Master's Thesis). Harvard University Press.

Wang, Y.M., & Chen, V.D.T. (2006). Untangling the confounding perceptions regarding the stand alone IT course. *Journal of Educational Technology Systems, 35*(2), 133-150.

Zheng, D., & Young, M.F. (2006). *Comparing instructional methods for teaching technology in education to preservice teachers using logistic regression, Methods for Teaching Technology in Education.* Proceedings of the 7th

International Conference of the Learning Sciences, Bloomington, Indiana.

Chapter 8

Using technology to assess students at a university in Tanzania: Lecturers' perspectives

Ezra Nathanael Ntazoya

Abstract

The purpose of this chapter is to explore the use of technology in assessing higher learning institution students at Archbishop Mihayo University College of Tabora (AMUCTA). The study used mixed research approach with descriptive research design. A sample of 83 participants were used in this study. The sample comprised the lecturers, support staff and students. Primary data of the study were gathered using semi-structured interviews, semi-structured questionnaires and group discussion schedules. Data were analysed descriptively using Statistical Package for Social Sciences (SPSS) and content analysis techniques. The findings indicated that, lecturers assess students using the prescribed assessment techniques. Both lecturers and the students are aware on the assessment tools used at higher learning institutions. The commonly used assessment tools include written examinations, written tests, written assignments and written quizzes. However, the tools are used with very little integration of technology to cope with the need 21st century driven curriculum. Results also revealed that, both lecturers and students need training on the applicability of various computer based skills essential for assessment process. This discrepancy pointed out led to address the need of using technology to make students assessment more effective. Perspective of lecturers involved in the assessment process formed the basis for analysis of the data gathered. Students' views were also important to complement the lecturers' views on the matter. It is recommended that, the college strive to improve its facilities that enhance assessment using technology. Additionally, in this century, assessment techniques used by instructors should be aligned to the current trends on technology and major innovations that could help both the instructors and students to do better in their teaching and learning endeavourers respectively.

Key Words: Curriculum; Assessment; Technology; Higher Learning Institution; Teaching and Learning

Introduction and Background

This chapter presents the concept of assessment in higher learning institutions in reference to Archbishop Mihayo University College of Tabora (AMUCTA). The background to the problem, problem statement, theoretical framework, and purpose of the study is presented. The significance of the study and research questions is also covered. Under methodology section, research design, data tools, population, sample and sampling procedures, data analysis plan and ethical issues have been considered. Findings of the study followed by discussion are also given. The paper ends with limitations and future research, conclusion and references.

Higher learning institutions are considered the place where the learners are expected to graduate with a repertoire of knowledge, skills and positive attitudes (Fuller, 2016). These can only be responded to, when the curriculum in use affords to provide the lecturers and students who implement the curriculum to get knowledge, skills and positive attitudes. Curriculum at higher learning institution is an important instrument that comprises the structures and layouts in which the body of knowledge is constructed during the process of its implementation (Boud & Falcikov, 2007). It provides among other things, the framework for assessing the students during their learning process.

The term assessment has simply meant the act of making judgment about something. Also, it is decision on the amount, value, quality or importance of something or the judgment or decision that is made (Mtibika, 2008). The term assessment has resulted in debate due to multiple definitions, purpose and its applicability particularly in higher education (Boud & Falchikov, 2009). Authors in the

Education Reforms (2015) asserts that, assessment is the wide variety of methods or tools that educators use to evaluate, measure, and document the academic readiness, learning progress, skill acquisition, or educational needs of students. In this study, the author has aligned the term assessment to various purposes, functions and forms. At higher learning institutions, assessment takes the form of high-stakes assessment at large. In Education Reforms (2015) the author contends that:

High-stakes assessments are typically standardized tests used for the purposes of accountability-i.e., any attempt by federal, state, or local government agencies to ensure that students are enrolled in effective schools and being taught by effective teachers. In general, high stakes means that, important decisions about students, teachers, schools, or districts are based on the scores students achieve on a high-stakes test. And either punishments (sanctions, penalties, reduced funding, negative publicity, not being promoted to the next grade, not being allowed to graduate) or accolades (awards, public celebration, positive publicity, bonuses, grade promotion, diplomas) result from those scores (Education Reforms, 2015 p.2).

Universities and University Colleges are in pressure to provide the market with highly competent graduates who are well qualified. At the same time, they are struggling to maintain the quality of education they provide. Besides, the assessment procedures have played a greater role in modeling the learning outcomes that mould the graduates from these universities and university colleges (Education Reform, 2015). While some authors have reported in favour of using the term assessment to refer to judging the students learning progress, yet, some studies show that, the term assessment has been used radically and traditionally and includes a lot of baggage in the past decade (Fuller, 2016). Fuller uses the word "evidence" or "inquiry" instead of assessment. To him, using the word assessment means teaching to test, the growing assessment culture of most of the growing and upcoming universities and university colleges in the world and Africa in particular.

Studies have shown that, educators and learners in young and growing universities and University College in Africa, Tanzania in particular are striving to attain the so-called "accountability-driven assessment" instead of learning-driven assessment (Fuller, 2016). Assessment should not be seen as a practice that should be done for one promotion. This is because, you find lecturers talking about the number of tests and any other assessment tools they administered per semester as part of the data to be filled in the Open Performance Review and Appraisal System (OPRAS) form. OPRAS forms are purely used for accountability and thus it is unfair to judge lecturers' performance based on how one has been assessing his or her learners. Fuller (2016) points out that, the fear to have penalties has an influence on the applicability of assessment as a tool for accountability. This implies that, educators may only be interested in the number of written test (high stake tests) or assignments given to students without comprehending the extent to which those tests served the purpose for students learning.

Another arena for discussion on assessment has been the way the faculty members are oriented to use the stipulated assessment tools in higher learning institutions. University owners and educational practitioners in Africa, particularly in Tanzania have overlooked for some years the way assessment is practised and how technology can be integrated in assessment process (Abdelmalak, 2016). Lecturers are not well oriented on the use, purpose, values and outcome of assessment. Boud and Falchikov (2007) contents that, instructors have just been using the traditional way of assessment without considering the new endeavourer from the students to be assessed.

Apart from being used as a tool for accountability, assessment practitioners ought to think about assessment and its implication to higher learning institutions. Fuller (2016) noted that, the thought may also be challenged by the fact that, lack of philosophy guiding educational assessment has been the common, yet, undermined problem in young universities and University College in Tanzania. It is high time for the assessors to think assessment in a more wide, yet, more technological way to get rid of a primitive and traditional kind of assessment. This can only be possible when there is use of technology in assessment. The uses of technology in assessment at higher learning institutions will make educators (mainly lecturers) re-define the term and make it more friendly to the learners by making them participate more in the assessment processes (Site et al., 2007).

This will make it easy for the learners to grasp knowledge and skills out of assessment practices as opposed to the current practices that make the students inferior and subjective to assessment procedures (Bates & Poole, 2003).

In Tanzania, higher learning institutions use technology not only in teaching and learning, but also in assessment of the students. Site and his colleagues (2007) contended that, the pedagogical and socio-economic forces that have driven the higher learning institutions to adopt and incorporate Information and Communication Technology (ICTs) in teaching and learning include greater information access; greater communication; synchronous and asynchronous learning; increased cooperation and collaboration, cost-effectiveness and pedagogical improvement. This entails that, universities and University College in Tanzania are striving to adopt and incorporate technologies in teaching and learning.

However, they noted that ICTs have not permeated to a great extent in many higher learning institutions in most developing countries due to many socio-economic and technological circumstances. This calls for an initiative that could boost the use of appropriate technologies not only in teaching and learning, but also in assessing the students to help them achieve the expected learning outcomes of the courses studied. Site and colleagues (2007) advovated the use of e-learning facilities that includes virtual labs, web based assessments, online testing, blended delivery methods involving collaboration software, mobile technologies, CDs and DVDs (CD-ROMS), online interaction software and computer based simulations.

This chapter discusses the uses of technology in assessing the students at higher learning institution. It specifically address the assessment tools used at AMUCTA, integration of technology in assessment (the extent to which technology is used), the knowledge required by both lecturers and students, challenges in the implementation of new technological inventions and the way forward to make use of technologies more successful.

Problem Statement

Assessment has been one of the difficult areas to deal with by both lecturers and students in many growing Universities in the world (Mtibika, 2008). Tanzania being one of the developing countries, her lecturers and students are also facing some difficulties in implementing assessment processes. Among other reasons, the complex nature of assessment has been due to its varied purposes (Wall, Hursh & Rodgers, 2014; Education Reforms, 2015). Despite the fact that technology is used in assessing the students, yet it is still not used appropriately to an extent of helping the students to achieve the expected learning outcomes with ease. While the central purpose of assessment is to weigh out the extent of the students' learnt knowledge; yet, the mechanism in which the same is given and administered has raised many questions to various educational practitioners.

Some of the questions are whether course instructors should use formal or informal assessment, whether more weight should go to formative or summative assessment, whether the validity and reliability of the tools used for assessment are adhered to and whether the appropriate technology is used in assessing the students. These have raised the questions on the lecturers' ability to convene assessment as a process in a more acceptable way and thus meet the expected students learning outcomes. Therefore, the study attempts to investigate the extent to which the uses of technology in assessing the students at AMUCTA have helped to bring effectiveness in the assessment process.

Theoretical Framework

This study adopted the variation theory to explain the need for higher education students to be part of the assessment process that the assessors are practicing. This is built in the foundation that, students are the key players in assessment that the assessors decide, as they are important part in its execution. Variation theory explains that individuals see, understand, and experience the world from their own perspectives (Cheng, 2016) .Therefore, students may not learn effectively if they are not aware of things in exactly the same way as the teacher (Lo, 2012 (in Cheng, 2016). However, the theory is suitable to improve learning by helping students develop their own ways to experience the phenomenon (or the object of learning).

Learning takes place when a student is "capable of being simultaneously and focally aware of other aspects or more aspects of a phenomenon" (Marton & Booth, 1997,p.142). Marton, et al. (2004,p.7) referred to this as "powerful ways of acting" being derived from "powerful ways of seeing". Lo (2012) supplements that teachers should help students develop "powerful ways of seeing" so that students can become more independent in dealing with new problems and issues in the future. The theory envisages that, for learning to occur, some critical aspects of the object of learning must vary while other aspects remain constant (Ho, 2014; Ko & Marton, 2004; Marton & Booth, 1997).

It further suggests that how students perceive a specific object of learning depends on what pattern of variations is provided by the teacher. It is expected that different patterns of variation result in different types of learning. According to Marton et al. (2004, p.16), there are four patterns of variation: contrast (i.e., recognizing values of an aspect), generalization (i.e., experiencing varied appearances of the same value), separation (i.e., separating aspects with varying values from invariant aspects), and fusion (i.e. experiencing several critical aspects simultaneously). Therefore, assessors must create the environment at which the students who are the one to be assessed to understand well the context to which the assessment is contextualized. Thus, the students should be aware, create meaning on the purpose of assessment, and make assessment more students based and more friendly. This will help to reduce the enmity between the assessor and students to be assessed.

Purpose of the Study

The purpose of the study was to investigate the extent to which the uses of technology in assessing the students at AMUCTA have helped to bring effectiveness in the assessment process. It specifically address the assessment tools used at AMUCTA, integration of technology in assessment (the extent to which technology is used), the knowledge required by both lecturers and students, challenges in the implementation of new technological inventions and the way forward to make use of technologies more successful.

Significance of the Study

Lecturers are the potential beneficies of the findings of this study in the sense that, they will be prompted to use technology when applying the prescribed assessment techniques to cope with technology driven curriculum for a 21st century student. At the college level, the findings will serve as a road map towards review of assessment techniques and procedures to enhance students learning. Furthermore, the findings of this study have built a strong foundation to assessors and researchers to have a threshold towards technological driven assessment in higher education.

Research Questions

The study was guided by the following main question:
How can technology be used in higher learning institutions to make students assessment more effective?

Methodology

The study used mixed methods approach with descriptive research design. This approach was used to allow the accommodation of both qualitative and quantitative paradigms. Descriptive research design allowed the author to collect primary data. Data were analysed using both descriptive statistical techniques and content analysis techniques. To have more descriptive details, the author ran Statistical Package for Social Sciences (SPSS) to get the friequencies and percentages. Jonson et al. (2007) points out that, studies that needs contextualized responses uses mixed methods research approach that takes into account the aspects of both qualitative research approach and quantitative research approach.

Research Tools

In this study, semi-structured interview guides were used to collect data from both lecturers and students. Interviews used helped the researcher get the inner conception on the usage of technology in assessing the students; and how such technology has been affecting them in achieving the expected learning outcomes. In addition, during the interview session, the respondents were given time to express their views in details that could not be obtained using the questionnaires. Both lecturers and students filled questionnaires with both open and closed ended questions. Questionnaires helped to get information from respondents that supplemented the information from interviews. The lecturers and students who filled the questionnaires were those who did not participate in the interview session. One group discussion with eight participants was conducted. This discussion session comprised of five students, a lecturer and two support staff. The themes for discussion were given to the members before the beginning of discussion. In this study, multiple tools for data collection was used to ensure that, data set complement one another and the researcher gets various angles of responses. Creswell (2003) asserts that no single technique or instrument may be considered adequate in collecting valid and reliable data. Thus, the tools triangulated each other to have full information from respondents about the topic studied.

Study Population

Archbishop Mihayo University College of Tabora (AMUCTA) as a college was taken to represent the young and growing Universities and University College in Tanzania. Teaching staff, non-teaching staff, support staff and students from AMUCTA formed the population of this study. The population of the categories mentioned from which the actual sample size was drawn is 570. This population was so important not only because the sample through which this study worked on, but also it reflected the nature from which the sample of the study was drawn.

Sample and Sampling Procedures

A sample of 83 participants drawn from a population of 570 participated in this study. 26 lecturers (23 Males, 3 Females) participated in the study. Among the 26 lecturers, 21 filled questionnaires, 4 participated in interview and 1 participated in group discussion. The study used few female lecturers because they are the only available by the time this study was being conducted. The study also used 2 support staff and 55 Bachelor of Arts with Education (BAED) and Bachelor of Education (Special Needs) (BEDSN) students. This sample of 83 participants was adequate and sufficed the data collection requirements of the study. Cohen, et al. (2002) indicates that, there is a need to careful select the research sample that is manageable and suffices the needs of the study. Table 1 indicates the sample size used in this study.

Table 1: Sample of the Study

Sample Category	Completed Questionnaires	Participated in Interview	Participated in Group Discussion	**Total**
Lecturers	21	04	01	**26**
Support Staff	-	-	02	**02**
Students	40	10	05	**55**
Total	**61**	**14**	**8**	**83**

Source: (Field Data, 2017)

In this study, a simple random sampling technique with the help of an agent (fellow lecturer with knowledge in ICT) was used to sample the lecturers from six departments available at the college. This helped the researcher to get the required sample with varied characteristics. Purposive sampling techniques were used to get both the lecturers and students who participated in the interview. Lecturers who were interviewed were only those considered to have additional knowledge in ICT application and had long experience in using computers than their counter parts. This ensured the researcher to get the authentic data from such respondents due to their experience. Students who filled questionnaires were sampled using simple random sampling techniques.

Respondents who participated in group discussion were also sampled purposively to ensure that they are the one having knowledge in the use of technology in assessing the students or they have experience with such assessment practices used at AMUCTA. This is because, the researcher's target was to get authentic information from the sampled respondents. The author decided to include a part time lecturer, students and technical support staff, to have a good combination of the respondents who participated in the discussion.

Data Analysis Plan

After data collection, data were organized and sorted into categories. Data collected using questionnaires were analyzed descriptively using Statistical Package for Social Sciences (SPSS). Data collected using interviews and group discussions was verbatimly transcribed and then analyzed using content analysis techniques. Content analysis technique was suitable because it helped to establish the categories of themes that made it possible to categorise the participants' responses during data analysis. Ary et al. (2010) proposed that, mixed research should bear various data analysis techniques to suit the data categories aligned to a certain technique of analysis.

Ethical Issues

Ethically, the author consulted the college research coordinator for endorsement of the data collection procedures. The purpose of the study was included in all the tools for data collection. This ensured transparency, validity and reliability of the data to be collected. The researcher sought participants consent before they actually involved in this study. A voice recorder was used only when the respondent agreed to be recorded. For the sake of maintaining anonymity of the respondents, the names of the respondents were not written in this chapter. Furthermore, the researcher observed all other ethical issues during the whole period of carrying out this study. This included the prior permission to conduct this study from the Deputy Principal-Academic Affairs (DPAA) and the University College Research Coordinator.

Results

The research project aimed at investigating the use of technology in assessing higher education students at AMUCTA. The focus was AMUCTA lecturers' perspectives. The study was guided by the following question; how can assessment in higher education use technology? To make the question meaningful, the following sub-questions were asked; what are the assessments tools used by lecturers in assessing students at higher education and to what extent do the assessment tools effectively integrated with technology? The findings of this study are presented using the following themes.

Lecturer and student awareness of key assessment tools

The researcher sought to know the awareness level of both lecturers and students on the assessment tools used to assess the students at higher learning institutions. The results indicate that, all 21 lecturers who filled questionnaires are aware on the assessment tools used to assess the students in higher learning institutions. On the key assessment tools used by lecturers to assess the students in their class in second semester of 2015/16 academic year, the results indicated that, 18 lecturers (90%) used traditional assessment tools while 3 lecturers (10%) used modern assessment tools(See Figure 1). Figure 1 indicates the results on the key assessment tools used by lecturers in their classroom in the last semester in 2015/16 academic year.

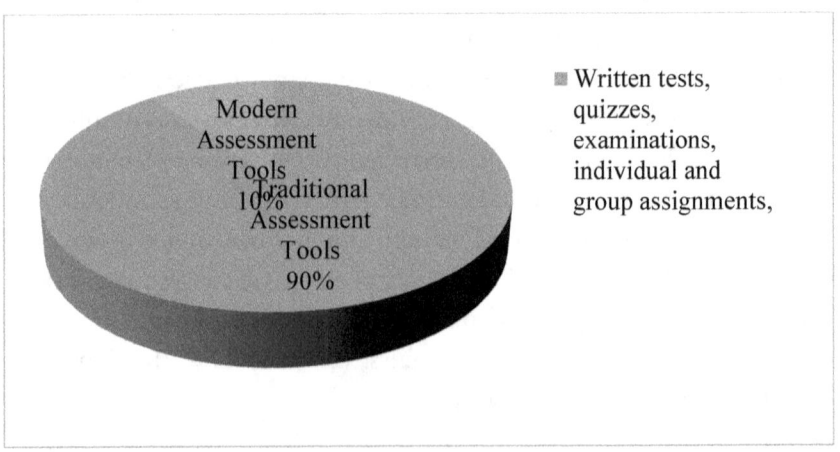

Figure 1: Assessment tools used by lecturers in 2015/16 academic year

Students' results indicate that, 38 students (95%) are aware of the assessment tools that the lecturer employ to assess the students at higher learning institution. Two students (5%) were not aware on the assessment tools used by lecturers. However, when required to name the key assessment tools used by the lecturers, the results indicates that, 37 students (98%) are aware with the traditional tools that include written tests, written quizzes, written examinations, and written assignments. On the other hand, only one student (2%) was aware with other modernized assessment tools that the lecturers used to assess the students. These included portfolios, projects, exhibition and oral comprehension exam that are linked with the use of ICT. The tools are referred as modern because they reduces the task of directly respond to the questions on the given answer sheet. They need a highly planed schedule to accomplish the assigned tasks and thus create role ship among the students.

Effectiveness of using technology in assessment to achieve expected student learning out comes

The results indicate that, all 21 lecturers (100%) agreed that the assessment tools could use technology to achieve the expected students learning outcomes. However, when the lecturers were asked to show how those assessment tools could use technology, the results indicate varied responses as indicated in Figure 2.

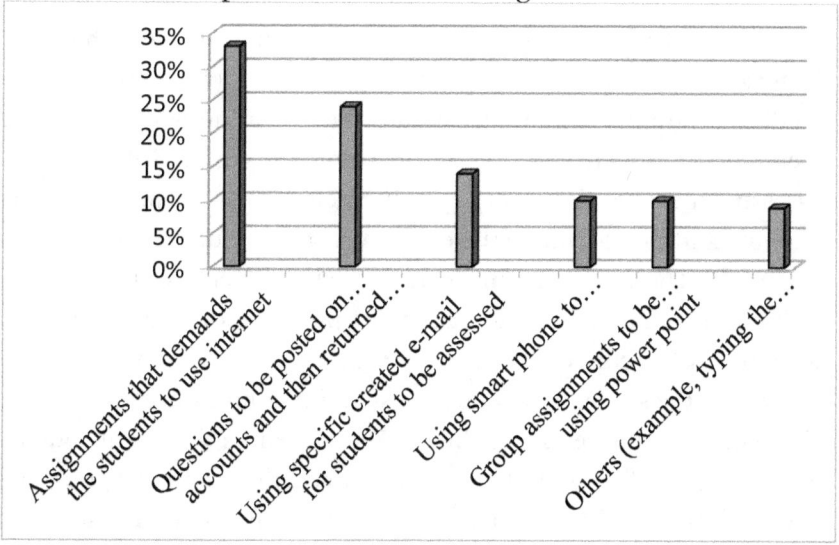

Figure 2: Results on how assessment tools uses technology at AMUCTA

Results on the extent to which students think their lecturers use technology in assessment indicated that, 99% agreed that the lecturers use technology in assesment. 1% said they do not use technology during assesment of the students. However, when they were asked on the same argument and how assessment can use technology, the results indicate that, they had varied views that are put in five categories as indicated in Figure 3.

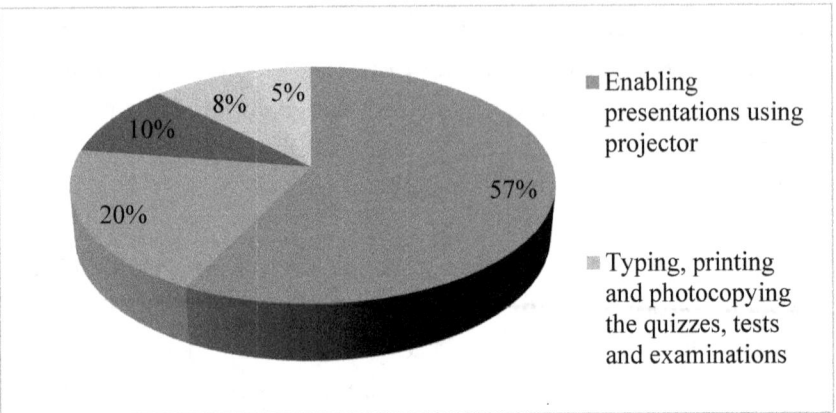

Figure 3: Students perspectives on the use of technology in assessment process at AMUCTA

The researcher as well sought to know the extent to which the lecturers use key technological advancement (mechanisms) for students learning. Under this issue, the results indicated that, 11 lecturers (51%) employ the mechanisms suggested for students' assessment and indicated how such mechanisms can help students learning and thus attaining the expected learning out comes (Refer to Figure 4). The suggested mechanism included using online testing, online examinations, online mailing of presentations and individual assignments, online quizzes, using projectors to present the lesson and assess the students, sending the students course tutorials through their accounts and returning the marked students assignments online. 10 lecturers (49%) did not respond to it and thus therefore, they did not indicate how some mechanisms could be used to assess the students learning. Figure 4 shows the extent to which the lecturers employ the suggested mechanism in students' assessment.

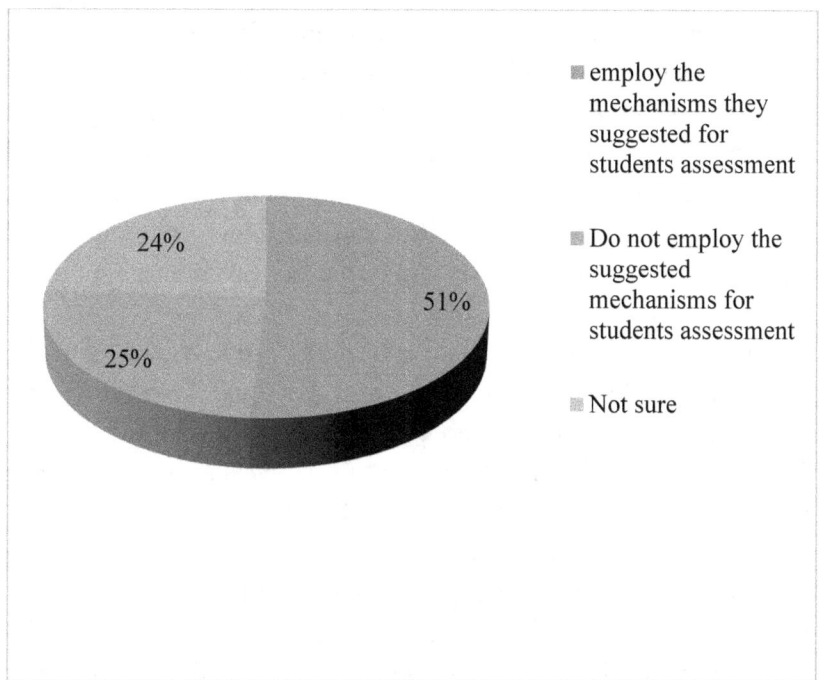

Figure 4: The extent to which the lecturers employ the suggested mechanisms for students' assessment

The results further indicate that, 39 students (99%) were aware that lecturers use various mechanisms to assess the students; however, they were not able to provide the essential contribution of such mechanisms to students learning and attainment of expected learning out comes. One student (1%) was not aware about the mechanisms used to assess the students at higher learning institutions.

Key knowledge needed by lecturers to conduct technology based assessment

The researcher needed to know the knowledge needed by the lecturers to conduct technology based assessment. The results indicate that, lecturers needs the use of technology in their assessment procedures, however, many of them do not have enough skills on the applicability of the suggested mechanisms to employ such technological skills. For example, when interviewed, one of the lecturers noted that: "It is important that lecturers use technology based assessment because most of them have laptops, but most of them do not have skills to support that technology".

When asked the extent to which the lecturers apply the suggested mechanisms in the process of assessment, the same respondent had the following to say: "Currently, the mechanisms suggested for lecturers to assess their students using technology are not well employed due to either lack of infrastructures or knowledge on the part of both instructors and students".

The study revealed also that, instructors see it is important for the University College to devise a system that can help the course instructors to teach using video conferencing especially for the part time lecturers who live in Dar es Salaam. However, instructors lack computer related skills that can make them fully employ the assessment procedures using technology at higher learning institutions. Therefore, computer orientation is necessary for effective implementation of assessment using technology.

Computer designed assessment on individual and group projects, exhibition, portfolios, demonstration, ICT based tests, simulations, case studies, executions and research based assessment need more knowledge on the part of course instructors. Such key knowledge may not be readily available among the instructors due to poor background on ICT. One of the lecturers commented that: "We may not end-up suggesting such mechanisms for assessing the students using technology, however, the question remain; are the lecturers equipped with such knowledge to cope with the current technology?".

Students had also the view that, course instructors need to be equipped with knowledge on computers that are essential in the applicability of technology in assessing the students. One of the students commented that: "There is great need for the improving technology knowledge to instructors and students so that to ensure the interaction between the media used and learners in teaching and learning process."

On the stressing of the importance of ICT know how, another student commented that: "Using technology in assessing the learners in higher education is what sometimes brings difference to other levels, and this has its importance in determining what the students can search and their actions on what they have learned".

Generally, the results from the interviewed students indicate that, there is a need to have a knowledge body for both the course instructors and the students before we can successfully embark on assessing the students using technology at higher education. This is built on the conception that, they have been seeing miss handling of assessment practices due to lack of experience in using technologies such as displaying a quiz, or exchanging the course materials given by their respective course instructors.

Curriculum enhancement for higher learning institutions assessment practitioners

The researcher sought to examine the extent to which the University College can reform her curriculum to suit the needs of students of this era. Lecturers were asked to comment on the extent to which the current curriculum satisfy them by providing the means through which they can assess the students using technology and how those means helps students learning?. One of the instructors commented that, "There is a need to equip both students and lecturers on basic computer skills that is now well explained how to get it from the curriculum (AMUCTA's Lecturer).

Another lecturer said that, "There is a need to train both the students and staff basics of computer and encourage them to use ICT in teaching and learning". He further suggested that, there is a need to introduce e-learning, where by students can interact with lecturers and with their courses online.

Perspectives for future implementation in using technology in assessment

The author sought to examine the respondents' general views on the use of technology in assessment in higher learning institutions. The respondents view that, 21st century students have to be assessed using not only the modern assessment tools that reduce them from written tests, but also using technological devise in the process of assessing the students. The curriculum used at higher learning institutions, AMUCTA in particular does not adequately provide room for the course instructors to devise the assessment tools that uses technology. However, this weakness of the current curriculum that is currently being worked on in the ongoing course review does not reduce the importance of using technology in students' assessment at AMUCTA. One lecturer who commented in group discussion said that:

ICT in assessment eases the work of lecturers, increases transparency and encourages students to have ICT skills. In Tanzania for example, many higher learning institutions are using ICT but to a lower level due to lack of infrastructure, technical knowhow and poor ICT background from family settings and from lower levels of education (primary and secondary).

Universities and University College should not be the victims of lack of technological (ICT) skills among its staff and students. This can be solved when the following suggestions given by technical support staff are worked on: "The use of ICT should not wait until one is in college or university. With currently available electricity, investments should be done into ICT in lower levels to build the culture of using ICT in learning and assessment."

Therefore, it is argued that, AMUCTA should build the culture of seeing technological innovations in teaching and learning particularly in assessment as part of university culture. This will not make course instructors victims of the assessment system that has not been integrated with technology in this digital age.

Discussion

This study aimed to investigate the use of technology in assessing higher learning institution students at AMUCTA. The focus was on lecturers' perspectives. The study was guided by the following question: How can technology be used in higher learning institutions to make students assessment more effective?

The researcher sought to know the awareness level of both lecturers and students on the assessment tools used to assess the students at higher learning institutions. The results indicate that, lecturers are aware on the assessment tools used in assessing the students at higher learning institutions. On the key assessment tools used by lecturers to assess the students in their class in the second semester in 2015/16 academic year, the results indicate that, lecturers used traditional assessment tools. This denote that, most of the lecturers used written test, quizzes, assignments, examinations and group assignments to assess the students in the last semester that they taught. This may not be healthy to knowledge gaining and attainment of the expected learning outcome on the part of the students in this age. Students need the tools that can build their capacity to create knowledge in their own (Education Reforms, 2015). Some assessment tools that can easily be integrated with technology and make assessment more effective include portfolios, focused dialogue, reflective essays, exhibitions, and case studies. These tools enabled the students to critically participate in the assessment process (Fuller, 2016).

Furthermore, students' results indicate that, they are aware with the assessment tools used by lecturers in assessment processes. These tools known are traditional and they were not able to establish the extent to which these assessment tools can be made more effective using technology. In addition, the fact that students failed to distinguish the traditional assessment tools and the modern assessment tools brings the assessment dialogue that entails more engagement of the students in the assessment process that how it is currently done at higher learning institutions. Modernized assessment tools that use technology need a highly planed schedule to accomplish the assigned tasks and thus create role ship among the students.

Fuller (2016) put it that, we need to have a national dialogue on the meaning and usage of assessment. This is because, if assessment is done in favor of the one who assess, then, assessment loses its meaning and purposes. This can be done through joint awareness procedures on the essence of assessment at higher learning institutions. This will help the students not to be subjects of assessments rather part of the key stake holder in the assessment process (Abdelmalak, 2016). Boud and Falchikov (2007) noted that, students are more favoring the assessment that reduces them from paper writing (examination type questions). They favor more the kind of assessment that will give them more freedom and thus more educative as they share experiences and knowledge.

Abdelmalak (2016) further comments that, adult students have a deep need to be self-directing; therefore, they resent and resist situations in which they feel others are imposing their wills on them. For example, exhibitions provide them with free time to exhibit what they have learned in class and thus show their creativity during exhibition of the various things in question. It creates the sense of role ship among the students and thus the use of technology could have eases this task, among others, to search for the materials to make exhibition successful. This calls for the ideas by Boud and Falcikov (2007) who instead on rethinking on assessment in higher learning institutions for the longer term.

The results on the effectiveness of using technology in assessment indicated that, various activities conducted at higher learning institutions could use technology. For example, conducting online lessons, presentations, creating lecturers-students interactive learning forums, submission of assignments online, discussion and searching learning resources online. The findings support the views by Katz and Macklin (2009) who stressed on the use of technology in higher learning assessments.

However, lecturers were in the view that, assessment can be done online and thus use more technology only if both instructors and students are well equipped with the ICT skills that can enable them to process the assignments online. With this view, the lecturers seem to be pessimistic. This is because; students are not well oriented on it as their lecturers. Thus, this results stress the importance of having internal and external capacity building on the teaching staff to enhance them to practice the modern assessment that uses technology that makes students part and not subject of assessment. Site et al. (2007) noted that, higher learning institutions are hampered by various pedagogical and technical challenges that make the students and faculty members to fail to effectively utilize the ICT resources available.

The results on the knowledge needed by lecturers in using technology to assess the students indicates that, lecturers needs the use of technology in their assessment procedures, however, many of them do not have enough skills on the applicability of the suggested mechanisms to employ such technological skills. It is unfortunate that, the fact that instructors lack major ICT skills and modern assessment skills tend to use the traditional assessment tools such as written tests, written examinations, written quizzes and group assignments. This is what Boud and Falchikov (2007) referred to as traditional assessment tools that can hardly lead to students learning in longer terms and hardly helps them to achieve the expected learning outcomes. It has been noted by Site et al (2007) that, instructors at higher learning institutions need the skills in managing e-learning and e-assessment.

This includes (but not limited to) designing the web based assessment activities, using multimedia assignment based, online testing, establishing computer communication practices and utilize virtual learning platforms when the university or college facilities allows that to be done. Furthermore, it has also some elements like online course management where both lecturers and students participate effectively in managing all the concern of the course online. At AMUCTA, despite the fact that the facilities are there, yet, some platforms such as using CD ROMS in assessing the students, dissemination of course materials and learning resources has not been done so far appropriately. This is what Selwyn (2007) called 'ICT is constructed in limited, linear, and rigid terms far removed from the creative, productive, and empowering uses which are often celebrated by educational technologists'.

The study findings revealed that, instructors see it important for the university college to devise a system that can help the course instructors to teach using video conferencing and other virtual learning facilities such as multi-media simulations, virtual labs, blended synchronous learning. This technology could have been more useful in assessing the students especially for the part time lecturers who live in various areas far away from Tabora region where the University College is located. This is currently a challenge not only because of instructors lack of computer related skills that could have supported that services, but also the curriculum in use rarely give room for such technical part to be implemented effectively.

In addition, the University College should strive to improve the use of technology in its departments and units by equipping them with not only internet-connected computers, but also Compact Discs (CDs), Digital Versatile Discs (DVDs), digital flash Discs (DFDs). For example, use of manual searching of the books in the library consumes students' time. This calls for curriculum reviews to accommodate the major changes that will take in the use of technology in students' assessment. Moreover, this calls for the University College to make some partnerships with other universities and make the university community built the culture of learning from other universities (benchmarking) on the use of technology in assessment of students. For example, the uses of moodle software, which can help the lecturers to make online course management. Site et al (2007) comments that, the use of such ICT facilities cannot be easily implemented, unless the lecturers are trained on how to handle and use such facilities at higher learning institutions.

It is obvious that both staff and students need to be equipped with ICT skills to share assessment implementation (Wall et al., 2014). The practice will increase computer literacy that in turn increases the way instructors use technology to assess the students (Katz and Macklin (2009). When both students and teaching staff are equipped with necessary skills, there is a possibility to devise e-learning strategies that support the use of online assessment tools. Universities and university colleges need to ensure that, there is readily available ICT facilities such as computers, projectors, Ipads, digital cameras, USB, memory cards,smart phone (few to mention) to ensure smooth students learning.

Limitations and Future Study

There are some limitations in the present study, and the ideas for future research noted below may address these limitations. First, some lecturers do not take it serious when it comes to research participation (however, it is well known participation is by one's consent). Thus, some did not return the questionnaires and no tangible reasons provided despite the fact that they were told several times. This delayed the processing of research data to meet the set deadline. Second, for the students, correcting data from them need a careful administration due to very tight schedule. Third, data from first year was very limited as they do not have experience on assessment; hence the researcher had to find some other students from second year and third year students to make the sample complete. Fourth, the findings of this study may be hardly generalizable to other higher learning institutions due to the nature of the sample. Only Bachelor of Arts with Education (BAED) and Bachelor of Education (Special Needs) (BEDSN) students participated in this study. Therefore, the results may not reflect the reality in other higher learning institutions in Tanzania. Future research may study the validity and reliability of assessment tools used for assessing the higher learning institution students and establishes the relationships for students' meaningful learning. This can help to break the gap of knowledge on authenticity of the assessment tools used in University and University Colleges in Tanzania.

Conclusion

This study provides some evidence for the uses of technology in students' assessment at high learning institutions in Tanzania, with reference to AMUCTA. The tools employed by the instructors in the assessment process have been detailed. The challenges exhibited in the use of technology in assessment of students have also been explained. This marks the beginning of the curriculum review that is in progress at AMUCTA to include the technological application in assessing the students to cope with 21st century curriculum driven requirements. In addition, there is a need to benchmark the pedagogical and technical skills in using technology to assess the students from other universities such as Sokoine University of Agriculture (SUA), Mzumbe University and Open University of Tanzania (OUT) which posses a well developed ICT facilities.

University of Dar es Salaam is more far with WEBCT and Blackboard, which are e-learning proprietary software. The aforementioned universities are having well established systems and applications (ICT facilities) on which technology is more effectively used than other universities in Tanzania. Our overall goal is to ensure that course instructors at higher learning institution uses technology in assessment and thus get rid from traditional assessment practices that has been commonly used for some years. Higher learning institutions are argued to set strategies to identify the best ways of integrating technology in assessment for the betterment of students learning and for the attainment of students expected learning outcomes.

References

Abdelmalak, M. M. (2016). 'Faculty-Student Partnerships in Assessment', *The International Journal of Teaching and Learning in Higher Education*, 28(2) ,193-203.

Ary, D., Jacobs, L. C., & Sorenes, C. K. (2010). *'Introduction to research in education'* (8th ed.). Belmont: Wadsworth.

Bates, A.W., & Poole, G. (2003). *'Effective Teaching with Technology in Higher Education: Foundations for Success'*. Indianapolis: Jossey-Bass.

Boud, D., & Falcikov, N. (Eds). (2007). *Rethinking Assessment in Higher Education Learning for the Longer Term:* London: Taylor and Francis Group.

Cheng, E. W. L. (2016). 'Learning Through the Variation Theory': A case study: *International Journal of Teaching and Learning in Higher Education*, 28(2), 283-292.

Cohen, L., Manion, L., & Morrison, K. (2002). *'Research methods in education'*. London: Routledge.

Creswell, J. W. (2003). 'Research Design: *Qualitative, Quantitative and Mixed Methods Approaches,'* (2nd ed). London: SAGE Publication.

Education Reforms. (2015), *'Assessment':* Retrieved from edglossary.org/assessment/

Fuller, M. B. (2016). *'Emerging Dialogue in Assessment: Meaning and Usage of Assessment (Part 1): Is it time for a new name for assessment'.* Retrieved from www.aalhe.org.

Hillary, H. S. (2016). 'The Strategy Project: Promoting Self-Regulated Learning through an Authentic Assignment, *International Journal of Teaching and Learning in Higher Education,*.28(2), 271-282.

Ismalim, O. F., & Koybasi, G. A. N. (2016). 'Use of Open educational Resources: How, Why and Why not,' *International Journal of Teaching and Learning in Higher Education*, 28(2), 230-240.

Jonson, R. B., Onwegbuzie, A. J., & Turner, L. A. (2007). 'Towards a Definition of Mixed Methods Research. *Journal of Mixed Methods Research*, 1(2), 112-133.

Katz, I. R., & Macklin, A. S. (2009). 'Information and Communication (ICT) Literacy: Integration and Assessment in Higher Education, *The Journal of Systemic, Cybernetics and Informatics*, 5(4), 50-55.

Mtibika, J. (2008). 'Curriculum and Assessment Frameworks: Can non-formal programmes benefit from these frameworks?' *Journal of Adult Education*, 16, 84-107. Dar es Salaam: Institute of Adult Education.

Nobert, M. (2012). '*Variation Theory: Encyclopedia of Science of Learning*'. Springer US. 3391-3393.

Owen. L. (2016). 'The Impact of Feedback as Formative Assessment on Students Performance, *International Journal of Teaching and Learning in Higher Education*, 282, 168-175.

Rutschow, E. Z., Grossman, A., & Cullinan, D. (2014). '*GED 21st Century-Learning Pathways: Pilot. Final Report. Mdvc*'. Retrieved from www.mdvc.org

Selwyn, N. (2007). 'The use of computer technology in university teaching and learning: a critical perspective' *Journal of Computer Assisted Learning*,23, 83-94. doi:10.1111/j.1365-2729.2006.00204.x

Site, A. S; Lwoga, E. T. and Sanga, C. (2007). 'New Technologies for Teaching and Learning: Challenges for Higher Learning Institutions in Developing Countries, Sokoine University of Agriculture, Tanzania', *International Journal of Education and Development Using ICT*. 3(2). Retrieved from http://ijedict.dec.uwi.edu/printarticle.php?id=246&layout=html

Wall, A. F; Hush, D. and Rodgers, J. W. (2014). 'Assessment for who: Repositioning Higher Education Assessment as an Ethical and Value-Focused Social Practice', *Journal of Research and Practice in Assessment*, 9(1),5-17.

Chapter 9

University Education and its impact on Nigerian technological advancement

Louis Okon Akpan

Abstract

In Nigeria, university education is designed to produce a high level of manpower for the economy. This study explores the impact university education has on Nigeria's technological advancement. For the study to be guided to its conclusion, the following roadmaps were developed: to examine various education policies initiated and implemented for the promotion of technology education, to examine the science and technology curriculum in Nigeria's universities and the impact of technology education has on the country's economy. Data generation was through the internet, newspapers, magazines and statistical publications from the relevant government offices. The data was analysed using thematic analysis. It was revealed from the findings that the policies enacted for the promotion of technology education are the information and communications technology policy, the admission policy, the science and technology quota policy and the private-sector participation policy. Furthermore, it was discovered that science and technology education impact on the Nigerian economy in the area of agriculture, oil and gas industries, solid minerals and mining, and the manufacturing sector.

Keywords: University education; Technological advancement; Education policies; Curriculum.

Introduction and Background

Universities all over the world are places where learning is sought at its maximum level and they are the centre for the production of high level manpower. Okoroma (2008, p.5) says:

> A university is different from other academic institutions because its preoccupation is not only in the diffusion of knowledge but in its extension. The university yearns for truth and subjects existing body of knowledge to critical examination and analysis to see if it needs revision. As a centre for excellence, universities are also expected to set the pace for the larger society in the efficient and effective management of human and material resources.

A modern university or what is known as university today evolved in the early 9th century in Salerno, Italy. However, the first university institution in Africa was established in Egypt during the 11th century and was referred to as *per-ankh* (Lulat, 2005). Within the West African context, it was not until 1934 that the West African elites in the persons of James Horton of Sierra Leone, Edwin Blyden, Casley Hayford of the then Gold Coast (Ghana) and Benjamin Azikiwe of Nigeria agitated for the establishment of university education in West African territory (Moti, 2010). The agitation prompted the then British Government to set up two independent commissions to look into the viability of the tertiary institutions in West African countries.

The two commissions unanimously agreed on the urgency and the ripeness of the need for the extension of university education to West African countries. In compliance with the recommendations of both the Asquith and Elliot Commissions, the foundation of the University College in Ibadan was laid in 1948 (Onokerhorage, 2000). The establishment of this institution notwithstanding, three others, the Universities of Zaria, Nsukka and Ife, were subsequently established after Nigeria's attainment of independence in 1960. It is documented in Nigeria's official government records that between 1960 and 1964, there were only 15 economists, 160 lawyers, 28 medical practitioners, 11 laboratory scientists and six agricultural scientists in Nigeria. However, there was no single qualified Nigerian in professions such as aeronautic engineering, automobile engineering, petroleum or chemical engineering, space science, soil science and nuclear science, among others.

Thus, as Coleman (2015) argues, during the process of decolonisation, university education was the instrument of politics in education that most nationalists used to gain popular support at the grassroots level. Therefore, there was an urgent need to provide the newly independent nations the needed manpower to jump-start the economy which was managed by the British before Nigeria's independence. In this study, however, effort is geared towards looking at the trends of development in university education in Nigeria. In addition, the study examines various education policies initiated and implemented for the promotion of technology education. Furthermore, the science and technology curriculum in Nigeria's universities and the impact of technology education on the country's economy are discussed. Before attempt is made to answer the questions above, we shall look at the purpose of university education within the contemporary Nigeria as highlighted in the Nigeria National Policy of Education.

The purpose of university education in Nigeria

The National Policy of Education (2004, p.38), which is the policy framework that guides the educational system in Nigeria, clearly stipulates the purpose of university education as follows:

a) Contribute to national development through high-level relevant manpower training.

b) Develop and inculcate proper values for the survival of the individual and the society.

c) Develop the intellectual capacity of individuals to understand and appreciate their local and external environments.

d) Acquire both physical and intellectual skills which will enable individuals to be self-reliant and useful members of the society.

e) Promote and encourage scholarship and community service.

f) Forge and cement national unity.

g) Promote national and international understanding and interactions.

Focus of the study

Science and technology education focuses on the training of technological personnel for the sole aim of initiating, facilitating and implementing the technological advancement of Nigeria, and it also creates the basic awareness of technological literacy among Nigerian youth. Science and technology education more than any other discipline, has more direct bearing on national welfare (Uwaifo, 2009). Therefore, this study focuses on the impact university education has on Nigeria's technological advancement.

Significance of the study

Since Nigeria attained political independence in 1960, it has recorded remarkable progress politically. In the context of technological advancement, one can equally say that the country has done well in this sector. This is because Nigeria has overcome its dependence on expatriates to drive the economy. Furthermore, the country's dependence on locally manufactured goods is a reflection of promotion of technology education by Nigerian leaders and policy makers. However, this study is of immense significance in so many ways. For instance, other developing countries in Africa will adopt Nigeria's initiative at ensuring that technology education is accorded importance because it is the engine room that drives the economy of a country. Having gone through literature, it was discovered that few scholars and researchers have written on technology education in the universities in Nigeria. In light of the above, this study not only contributes to existing scholarship, but it will act as a resource for other researchers in education.

Theoretical framework

This study is anchored on human capital theory which was propounded by Adam Smith and extended by Gary Becker. The essence of this theory is that investment is made in human resources so as to improve their productivity and also their earnings (Becker,

Cinnirella & Woessmann, 2012). In other words, the theory rests on how education increases the productivity and efficiency of workers by increasing the level of cognitive stock of economically productive human capability which is a product of innate abilities and investment in human beings (Olaniyan & Okemakinde, 2008; Akhuemonkhan, Raimi & Sofoluwe, 2013). Similarly, de la Fuente (2011) opines that human capital and growth are built around the hypothesis that the knowledge and skills embodied in humans directly raise productivity and increase an economy's ability to develop and to adopt new technologies. Here, western education is seen as an asset which by itself is productive.

From all indications, an educated population is a productive population. Supporting this assertion, a study conducted by Khan (2014) and Baruch and Lavi-Steiner (2015) indicates that a ten percent increase in education produced a growth of three percent in labour productivity. If education can raise workers' productivity, it then follows that university education would likely affect firms' aggregate output by tenfold. In line with the theory's argument, the assumption is that the Nigerian government's high investment in university education does not only have a corresponding increase in labour productivity, but it also reflects significantly on the country's technological sector. Therefore, the theory is used as a lens to unpack the level of Nigeria's technological advancement occasioned by the establishment of university education.

Methodology

This study used a qualitative approach. Silverman (2016) argues that the quality of any study is dependent and enhanced by a solid research design. The reason for the location of the study within the qualitative approach is, as Tuckman and Harper (2012, p. 45) argue: "directed towards providing the interpretative explanations that help to illuminate an understanding of social phenomena." However, the strength of a qualitative approach lies in an in-depth understanding of the social phenomenon under investigation (Cohen, Manion & Morrison, 2013). In line with the qualitative approach, interpretive paradigm was employed to investigate ways in which university education impacts on Nigerian technological advancement. Myers (2013) argues that the premise of interpretive scholars is that access to reality (whether given or socially constructed) is only through social constructions such as language, consciousness and shared meanings.

In the study, the purposive sampling technique was used. According to Saunders, Lewis and Thornhill (2012), purposive sampling is a sampling technique in which the researcher relies on his or her own judgment when choosing members of the population to participate in the study. In light of the fact that this is a desktop study where information on the topic under investigation abounds on the internet, it is therefore appropriate to judgementally select the materials that would best answer the research questions.

Data was generated using desktop search materials. Cardarelli (2008) says that desktop study looks at the research information which is generated without necessarily going to the field. The information was generated through existing resources such as newspapers, the internet, analytical reports and statistical publications (Ausburn & Ausburn, 2004). For clarity purposes, data on the development in Nigerian university education, different education policies initiated for technology education between 1948 and 2016, curriculum of technology education and the impact of technology education on Nigeria's economy was generated from the internet. It is worthy to mention that data generated spans between 1948 and 2016. The reason for the choice of the period 1948 and 2016 was because 1948 was the year the university institution was first established in Nigeria. Furthermore, 2016 was the year the federal government of Nigeria through the National Universities Commission gave operational licenses to individuals, organisations and states to establish university institutions.

In order to make sense of the rich information that was generated, open coding was used. Thematic analysis was employed to analyse the emerging themes. In other words, analysis for the study followed an inductive approach of theme identification, which began with the derivation and application of a thematic protocol. Furthermore, it followed a systematic process of interpretative synthesis as an alternative to the deductive application of a predetermined analytical framing (Weed, 2008). In addition, the nature and structure of the domain was determined through the identification, organisation and classification of data. Accordingly, the themes identified denote the core ideas and arguments on which this study's research questions, constructs and concepts are based.

Results

Development of university education in Nigeria

Understanding Nigerian universities necessitates the need to explore the historical background of university education in Nigeria in order to appreciate the salient issues raised in this study (Arowolo & Ogunboyede, 2012). From the findings, it was established that in the 1999 Nigerian Constitution, university education is placed under the concurrent legislative list, which means that the federal, state governments and private individuals have the power to establish and run university education. From the 1970s to today, these two tiers of governments and some private individuals/organisations have doubled in their efforts to provide accessible and quality university education to Nigerians and foreigners.

According to the National Universities Commission (NUC) (2016), there are 265 universities in Nigeria. It was revealed that NUC is an agency which was established in 1962, under the Federal Ministry of Education (FME) as an advisory agency in the cabinet office by Decree No. 1.1974. This commission is empowered to advise on the creation of new universities and other degree granting institutions, distribute government grants in accordance with a set formula, collect, analyse, and furnish information relating to university development and education in Nigeria, and act as the agency for channelling all external aid to Nigerian universities.

In addition, the commission is charged with the responsibility of ensuring an orderly development of university education, the maintenance of high standards, and the avoidance of unnecessary and wasteful duplication of academic programmes, faculties and facilities (Kanyip, 2013). From all indications, the establishment of the

universities in Nigeria can be grouped into generational phases namely:
a) First generation universities, 1948-1970
b) Second generation universities, 1971-1978
c) Third generation universities, 1979-1980
d) Fourth generation universities, 1981-1999
e) Fifth generation universities, 2000-2016

Universities such as Ibadan, Nsukka, Ife, Zaria, and Lagos are regarded as the first generation universities as their establishment was based on the need to replace colonial masters with Nigerians to control both the economic, administrative and political positions in the country. Babalola (2014) argues that during this period, universities in Nigeria were under the close surveillance of the regional governments (Western, Northern, Eastern and Lagos governments). In spite of the fact that these universities were under the close surveillance of the regional governments, their curriculums were not technologically based. Therefore, their products were 'brewed' mainly for the administrative positions.

Second generation universities are Calabar, Ilorin, Jos, Sokoto, Maiduguri, Port Harcourt and Ado Bayero University, Kano, which were established between 1971 and 1978. The essence of the establishment of these universities was because of the third national development plan (1975-1980) which was aimed at achieving both economic and social progress in Nigeria. Ugwuanyi (2014) states that aside from achieving economic and social progress for the country, the third national development plan also focused on expansion of agriculture, industry, transport, housing, water supply, health facilities, education, rural electrification, community and state programmes. Just like the first generation universities, second generation universities were not science or technology-oriented.

Universities which fall into the category of the third generation universities are Imo State University, Ondo State University, Lagos State University, Oyo State University of Technology, Ogun State University, Cross-River State University and Edo State University. It is worthy to say that these universities were established and administered by different state governments (Anyamelle, 2004). Additionally, the establishment of these universities was not based on the manpower needs of the states. Rather, their establishment was politically motivated since the founding fathers were politicians. Adesola (2002) states that politicians decided to exploit the placement of university education on the concurrent legislative list to prosecute their various election manifestoes in relation to education. Nyewusira (2014) says that all the preceding historical portrayals establish that political expedience or convenience was an overwhelming factor in the founding of state universities. Meanwhile, the curriculum of these universities was generic hence it did not focus on the immediate challenges faced by the states. In other words, it means that the products from these universities are completely irrelevant to the manpower needs of the state which is manpower for industrialisation.

It was discovered that between 1981 and 1999, the then federal military government of Nigeria, realising the need for industrialisation of the country through scientific and technological applications, established science and technology universities in six geopolitical zones. The universities are: Federal University of Technology, Akure, Federal University of Technology, Yola, Federal University of Technology, Bauchi, Federal University of Technology, Minna, Federal University of Technology, Abeokuta and Federal University of Technology, Owerri. The location of these universities was based on the availability of certain mineral resources that needed to be exploited using products of these universities. In other words, the locations where six of the universities were situated are all endowed with one natural resource or another. However, the curriculum was designed in line with the needs of the people. According to Akindele (2013), these universities develop at every stage of the education system, a scientific and technological attitude in preparation for the country's technological take-off.

Findings indicated that the fifth generation universities may be regarded as an era of deregulation of university education in Nigeria. According to Ajayi and Ekundayo (2008), deregulation of university education refers to breaking the government's monopoly of the provision and management of university education by giving free rein to private participation in the provision and management of university education in the country. In recent times, the federal government of Nigeria has given operational licenses to private individuals and organisations to establish university education. This is done in order to complement governmental efforts at providing university education to Nigerians and foreigners.

As of November 2016, there are about 81 approved private universities in Nigeria. Despite the private involvement in the establishment of university education, the federal government within this period founded eight Federal Universities of Science and Technology. From the interpretive perspective, the reason for the establishment of these eight universities by the federal government is for geo-political balancing. It is worthy to say that before now some states in Nigeria were not accommodated in the provision of a federal university. Nyewusira (2014) observes that while federal government was bent on geo-political balancing of federal universities, the states and their governors were also engrossed in the political zests to have their own universities within this period. This phenomenon no doubt had its attendant implications for the trend of university expansion in the country.

Policies for promoting technology education

Nigeria has the largest number of universities in sub-Saharan Africa (Clark, 2013). Findings showed that Nigeria has a total student population of 2 356 038 in its universities. Out of this number, approximately 43.8% of the students are in the science and technology-related disciplines (NUC, 2015). Because of the low enrolment figure in areas, the federal government of Nigeria through one of its agencies (NUC) came out with various policies to arrest the trend. The policies enacted for promotion of technology education are as follows: the Information and Communications Technology (ICT) policy, the admission policy, the science and technology quota policy and the private-sector participation policy.

Information and communications technology (ICT) policy

It was established that in Nigeria the implementation of the ICT policy began in April 2001 after the Federal Executive Council approved establishment of the National Information Technology Development Agency (NITDA) which is saddled with the responsibility of implementing the policy. Findings showed that the ICT policy was enacted in order to ensure that every student and lecturers alike in Nigerian universities not only have a personal computer but were able to use these for e-learning and literature searches for teaching and research. Matthew, Joro and Manasseh (2015) argue that the essence of the introduction of ICT in Nigerian universities is:

a) To support collaborative research among Nigerian universities, research and higher educational institutions (in addition to collaborative research with others).

b) To train a pool of ICT engineers, scientists, technicians, and software developers in order to increase the availability of trained personnel in Nigeria.

c) To provide attractive career opportunities particularly in the area of science and technology.

d) To develop requisite skills in various aspects of ICT.

However, in realising the importance of ICT application in national development, it was maintained that the acquisition of basic ICT skills and capabilities have recently been made mandatory by NUC as part of the national minimum standard for first degree in Nigerian universities. Agyeman (2007), Matthew, Joro and Manasseh (2015) assert that the demand for computer/ICT literacy is increasing in Nigerian universities because employees and employers have realised that computers and other ICT facilities do enhance efficiency in the workplace.

Admission policy

From the findings, the admission policy is another channel through which the federal government of Nigeria, through its agency 'Joint Admissions and Matriculation Board (JAMB)' tries to encourage Nigerians to offer science and technology-related disciplines in the universities. JAMB was created by Decree number 2 of 1978 with the sole responsibility of streamlining admissions and expanding access to universities. The board came out with a policy which allows students to be admitted into universities based on four criteria: merit, catchment area, educationally disadvantaged areas/states and university discretion (Okebukola, 2006). Students admitted on merit must be 40%, 30% of the total admissions is assigned to catchment area, 20% to educationally disadvantaged groups and 10% to university discretion (Adeyemi, 2001). The stratification and categorisation of candidates for admission into the universities in Nigeria equally enhance access to science and technology-related disciplines. This is because students from deep rural areas who were not 'privileged' to be admitted for these disciplines due to distance were accommodated in this new arrangement. The introduction of the admission quota policy was motivated by demand for an increase in access and participation in science and technology education by all strata of the country.

Science and technology quota policy

From the findings, it was discovered that the science and technology quota policy came into existence when the federal government of Nigeria realised that universities are admitting and also graduating people who are looking at the government for employment. Official records from the Federal Ministry of Labour and Employment and the National Bureau of Statistics indicated that since Nigeria's independence, universities in the country had produced over 85% graduates in liberal arts and humanities, while 15% were in the science and technology disciplines. Realising this lop-sidedness in the production of graduates, NUC gave directive that all universities in the country should admit 60% science and technology students and 40% liberal arts and humanities students (Chukwurah, 2011).

The implication of this is that thousands of science and technology applicants who failed to be admitted because of limited spaces were accommodated. From all indications, although the above policy resulted in the increment of candidates in science and technology disciplines, it may have allowed for poorly qualified students to be admitted into Nigerian universities. This assertion is supported by Kanyip (2013) who argues that using the quota system to guide and regulate access to university education has the inequitable consequence of reducing the chances of admission for highly qualified applicants. The outcome of this policy has always been catastrophic because meritocracy tends to be subverted and thus less qualified people are admitted (Kanyip, 2013).

Private sector participation policy

The data analysed indicated that the increasing costs of training and producing graduates in science and technology-related disciplines in universities have prompted government to seek alternative ways of financing the programmes. It was also found that a combination of enrolment pressures in these disciplines, resistance of institutions to adapt more efficient and productive financial management styles by authority of various universities, and inability of government to keep pace with cost pressures in the face of other competing social demands, have forced government to have a rethink of the exclusive funding of science and technology education (Bello, 2012). In light of the above, a cost sharing measure was developed and adopted, this was known as the private sector participation policy.

Findings showed that this policy was aimed at inviting other stakeholders to participate in funding science and technology-related disciplines. For instance, oil companies such as Nigeria National Petroleum Corporation (NNPC), Shell Petroleum Development Company Nigeria Limited, Nigeria Liquidified Natural Gas (NLG) Ltd, among others, were found to have annually invested heavily in science and technology programmes in some selected universities of technology in Nigeria. Furthermore, it was asserted that the federal ministries and parastatals such as the Federal Ministries of Works and Transport, Housing, Water Resources, Health and Science and Technology have all been involved in the funding of science and technology programmes.

In the 2015 academic year, official record from the NUC shows that over 2 593 students were given scholarships to pursue different technology disciplines in some universities in Nigeria This finding is in line with the position held by Akpan and Undie (2007) that the socio-economic hardship which deprived many students of the opportunity to attend university because they do not have enough money to pay for their tuition fees, is salvaged by these multinational companies and ministries which provide billions of naira annually to cater for their educational needs.

Curriculum of technology education in universities

Ocholla (2003) conceptualises curriculum as a fundamental part of any education or training programme largely because it provides not only a list of courses or modules offered in a programme, but it also gives appropriate information on the content, purpose, method, time/duration and location or situation of a programme or course, all of which are essential in a successful dispensation of manpower training and education. In Nigeria, it was discovered that NUC is saddled with the responsibility of designing and developing the curriculum for all universities. All programmes offered by different universities in Nigeria are centrally designed. Furthermore, it was revealed that the time/duration for each programme, the contents, manpower and materials specified are expected to be the same in all universities offering that programme. However, whether the specified requirements are made available by each university remains debatable.

In the context of science and technology disciplines, NUC came out with a dynamic and people-oriented curriculum. In order to produce sound and all-round graduates who are capable of turning around the country's economy through technology, the duration for any programme in science and technology disciplines was increased from four to five years. In other words, students studying science and technology disciplines are mandated to spend a minimum of five years or a maximum of nine. Similarly, before graduation students are required to embark on a one-year internship programme in an organisation in order to orientate and acquaint themselves with practical skills needed in the real-world situation. Additionally, findings indicated that students are allowed to spend about 60% on theoretical work in the classroom, while 40% is reserved for laboratories or workshops for the practical side.

Furthermore, the curriculum contents of science and technology disciplines are heavily loaded with local content. For instance, from data analysis it was established that in the School of Agriculture and Agricultural Technology of the Federal University of Technology, courses like fish post-harvest technology, crop processing and storage and farm power machinery are introduced in order to equip students with skills on how to use solar energy which is in abundance in Nigeria to process and store agricultural produce.

In the area of imparting knowledge, it was found from the study that the conventional method in which lecturers transfer knowledge to students through reading out lesson notes to them to take down has been replaced by group-collaborative learning which is more practical-oriented. In group-collaborative learning situations, students do not simply assimilate new ideas. Rather, they generate new ideas by working actively with them. However, the availability of internet services significantly helps group-collaborative learners to receive immediate, unambiguous and meaningful feedback from the lecturers. Supporting the above assertion, Zhu (2012) states that internet-supported collaborative learning promotes meta-cognitive processes, reflective interaction and problem solving. This section discusses the positive impact university education has had on Nigerian technological advancement in recent years.

Science and technology education and Nigerian economy

Science and technology education is widely acknowledged as a leading instrument for promoting economic growth. In Nigeria, science and technology has positively influenced all sectors of the economy. In other words, Nigerian economic prosperity is entirely dependent on science and technology advancement. Although the impact of science and technology on the Nigerian economy is felt in many sectors, because of limited space in this article, effort is made to tease out within the context of agriculture, oil and gas industries, solid minerals and mining, and the manufacturing sector.

Improvement in agricultural production

Apart from hydrocarbon, of which Nigeria is the sixth largest exporter of crude oil and has the second largest deposit of natural gas in the world, the country has a comparative advantage in the agricultural sector. It is pertinent to say that varieties of crops and animals are produced and reared respectively because of the favourable climatic condition and good soil structure. It was established by Oyedepo (2014) that over 70% of the entire land mass of the country is arable, however, only about 48% is presently been cultivated. Findings showed that before the year 2001, agriculture in Nigeria was dominated by small-scale farmers who produced about 85% of food requirements needed in the country. Although these farmers applied their physical energies for the cultivation of crops, the resultant yields were very limited.

The poor yields recorded were as a result of their inability to apply science and technology innovation in the planting and harvesting of crops. Records from the National Bureau of Statistics indicated that small-scale farmers in Nigeria produced about 16% rice per hectare between 1975 and 1992. The unimpressive performance in agricultural yields despite the amount of physical energy exerted was as a result of non-application of technology in the cultivation of the crops, which lead to poverty among local farmers in Nigeria.

It was found that the Federal Government of Nigeria in recent times introduced mechanised agriculture to revamp the agricultural sector and ensure food security, and job creation, to diversify the economy and enhance foreign exchange earnings. Similarly, findings indicated that modern agricultural technology has contributed positively to agricultural development in the country. The gap between developed countries and Nigeria in the area of agricultural production can be attributed largely to differences in the level of technological development, adaptation and transfer process (Odebode, 2014). It is worthy to mention that due to adoption of science and technology in the agricultural sector, food production and processing has been improved in recent times. However, it was reported by the current Minister of Agriculture (Dr Audu Ogbeh) that the non-oil export sector has been growing in the past five years because of the adoption of technology in the agricultural sector.

In the context of agricultural biotechnology, the global demand for alternative energy has opened up the market for bio-fuel which has consequently created opportunities for entrepreneurs in agricultural business in Nigeria. In addition, the production of ethanol fuel from cassava, jatropha plant, sunflower, and sugarcane, among others, is the impact science and technology education brought to the country's economy. From all indications, it will not be out of place to conclude that the improvement witnessed in the agricultural sector in Nigeria is a reflection of the turn-out of graduates from universities in agriculture technology-related disciplines.

Indigenisation of oil and gas industries

Findings indicated that Nigeria is the second largest producer of oil and gas in the world. The country's oil and gas industry has been vibrant since the discovery of crude oil in 1956 by the Shell Group (KPMG, 2014). Data analysis showed that until the late 1990s the sector was largely dominated by multinational corporations. In other words, the oil and gas sector in Nigeria was monopolised by foreign companies who hired foreigners in key sectors of the industry. It was revealed that before now, Nigerians were only employed as cleaners, tea girls, security personnel and clerical staff. The reason for the employment of Nigerians to junior positions was that they were not competent and skilful enough to be saddled with the huge responsibilities that the sector demands. By implication, Nigerians were not employed in key sectors of the industry because they did not have the technological know-how.

In 1999, the government's realisation of non-employment and utilisation of skilled Nigerians in this sector necessitated the introduction of indigenisation and local content policy. Findings showed that the policy allows for the participation of Nigerians in the oil and gas sector of the economy. In addition, local participation was boosted with the implementation of the Nigerian Content Directives (NCD) issued by the Nigerian National Petroleum Corporation (NNPC) about a decade ago. NCD is aimed at promoting a framework that guarantees active participation of Nigerians in oil and gas sectors without compromising standards. In other words, the essence of NCD is to transform the oil and gas sectors into the economic engine for job creation and national growth by developing in-country capacity and indigenous capabilities.

In order to actualise the targets and objectives of NCD, indigenous companies, local engineers, welders, local manufacturers of steel plates and pipes were allowed to participate both in upstream and downstream sectors. Currently, various indigenous oil companies such as Atlantic Energy, Addax oil, Agip Energy, Brass Exploration, Star Deep Water Petroleum, Amalgamated Oil, among others, are actively participating in oil exploration in Nigeria. Furthermore, many private organisations and individuals were recently granted operational license to establish oil refineries. For instance, the first largest indigenous oil refinery (Dangote oil and petrochemical company) is near completion. On completion, it will be the largest oil refinery in Africa, moreover, it was discovered that the refinery has the potential to satisfy Nigeria's daily requirement of 445 000 to 550 000 barrels of fuel, with spare capacity for exportation.

Nigerian National Petroleum Company (NNPC) Bulletin of 2015 indicated that indigenous oil companies are producing close to 45% of the total oil and gas in Nigeria. Additionally, it was reported that government directed that the indigenous companies should ensure that about 75% of the materials used in the exploration of oil and gas must be locally sourced or are of local contents (NNPC Bulletin, 2015). In this study, local content refers to the quantum of composite value added to or created in Nigeria through utilisation of Nigerian resources and services in the petroleum industry resulting in the development of indigenous capability without compromising quality, health, safety and environmental standards. It was revealed that the local content is framed within the context of growth of Nigerian entrepreneurship and the domestication of assets to fully realise Nigeria's strategic developmental goals.

Based on the Local Content Scheme (LCS) of government, records from the National Bureau of Statistics indicated that 160 000 local engineers were employed in the oil and gas industry in Nigeria between 2008 and 2014. Similarly, over 125 070 artisans trained in technology education were recruited into various oil and gas companies (National Bureau of Statistics, 2016). In the same vein, during the 2014 fiscal year, over 71.8% of local materials were locally sourced and used in the oil and gas sector. Data analysed indicated that indigenous service companies have asked to be involved in the construction of the $14 billion Dangote Oil Refinery as a way of avoiding enormous capital flight from Nigeria. When translated into monetary terms, it shows that the country will save over three trillion naira in foreign exchange. From the above, it was evident that university education in Nigeria has positively impacted on technological growth in the oil and gas sectors.

Solid minerals and mining industries in Nigeria

From the data analysis, it was discovered that one of the gains derivable from science and technology education is the participation of skilled Nigerians in the mining sector. Nigeria is blessed with abundant solid mineral resources. Coal, limestones, iron ore, copper and columbites are produced in large quantities in Nigeria. Like in the oil and gas industry, these mineral resources were predominantly monopolised by foreign companies before 1990. Expatriates and other skilled workers were brought in from America, Germany, Britain, Russia and France to work on these mines. There was capital flight from Nigeria to the developed world, not only in the area of exportation of raw materials but also on the issue of employment of foreigners. Supporting the assertion, Okorafor (2014) argues that specialisation in export production leads to distortion or disarticulation of the domestic economy, thus preventing balanced growth in Nigeria.

Aside from the Nigerian government establishing a Ministry with specific focus on mineral development in 1995, it also introduced a mineral policy in 1997. Findings indicated that the government promulgated the Minerals and Mining Decree in 1999 and conducted a major policy review through the Presidential Committee on Solid Minerals Development in 2003. The mining reforms were put in place by the federal government to address the policy failures of the past and open the mining sector up to a wave of indigenous private sector investment. It is worthy to note that mining companies such as Delta Steel Company, National Iron Ore Mining Company, Oke-Ila Orangun Mining Company, Tongyi Allied Mining, Kogi Iron Mines, among others, in spite of the complexity of technology, engaged young and skilled Nigerians turned out from Nigeria's universities in technology-related disciplines. From all indications, it is not out of place to say that the employment of technologically trained Nigerians in the solid mineral sector help to combat poverty in Nigeria, and also boost Nigeria's dwindling economy which has nosedived into recession due to mismanagement.

Manufacturing sector

Nigeria has an estimated population over 182 million people (www.population.gov.ng). Apart from being one of the most populous nations in Africa, Nigeria is Africa's largest economy and is worth more than $500 billion and $1 trillion in terms of nominal GDP and purchasing power parity respectively (www.population.gov.ng). It was evident from the data analysis that the country's manufacturing sector is one of the main driving forces behind the country's economic growth. The food, beverage and tobacco sectors are the most important and account for more than half of the nominal factory output. In addition, textiles, apparel and footwear are the second largest contributors to the country's economy. Furthermore, it was established that the automobile, chemical and pharmaceutical sectors apart from growing by 38.5% in 2015, contribute about 12% to the total country's GDP.

The manufacturing sector witnessed a strong growth in Nigeria in recent years. It was discovered from the analysis that there were steady increases in the Nigerian economy of 6.55% in 2010, 7.79% in 2011 and 2012, 9.03% in 2013, 11.6% in 2014 and 15.3 % in 2015. This finding was supported by Nevin, Akinbiyi and Nwokoneya (2016) who reported that the growth in the non-oil sector has been the main driver of Nigeria's economic growth and employment. Despite the fact that it was discovered that this steady growth was occasioned by a favourable business climate created by the federal government of Nigeria, it was also found that the availability of skilled man-power produced by the universities in technology-related disciplines significantly assist in no small measure in creating the necessary impact on the economy. In summary, it was found that the manufacturing sector provides the greatest opportunity for the transformation of the Nigerian economy through employment, creation of wealth and threshold for sustainable development.

Conclusion

Within the scope of this study, it is rather impossible to present the full picture of the impact of technology education on the Nigerian economy. However, it was possible to argue that an astronomical growth witnessed in university education in Nigeria since the 1970s has also shown a corresponding growth in the country's technological advancement. Based on a sound science and technology curriculum, Nigerian universities have been able to produce graduates who are technologically endowed to re-engineer the economy for better productivity. Technology education unarguably emerged as the dominant force in determining the wealth of a nation. The IMF chairperson predicted that despite the current economic recession, the Nigerian economy will witness double digit growth in 2017. The prediction was not only based on sound economic policies initiated by the current civilian administration lead by President Mohammedu Buhari, but it was necessitated by the availability of young skilful engineers, scientists and entrepreneurs produced by the country's universities.

References

Adesola, A. A. (2002). The State of Education in Nigeria. In Hubert J. Charles and Emeka Iheme (Eds.). Nigerian Private Sector and Education for All, UNESCO.

Adeyemi, K. (2001). Equality of access and catchment area factor in university admissions in Nigeria. *Higher Education, 42*(3), 307-332.

Agyeman, O.T. (2007). ICT for Education in Nigeria. *Survey of ICT and education.* Abuja: Government Publishers.

Anyambele, S. C. (2004). Institutional Management in Higher Education; A Study of Leadership Approaches to Quality Improvement in University Management. Nigerian and Finish Cases. *An unpublished Ph.D. Thesis submitted to the Department of Education, University of Helsinki.*

Akhuemonkhan, I. A., Raimi, L. & Sofoluwe, A.O., (2013). Entrepreneurship education and employment stimulation in Nigeria. *Journal of Studies in Social Sciences*, 3(1), 45-62.

Akindele, I. (2013). Evolution of private universities in Nigeria: Matters arising and the way forward. *Educational Research and Reviews*, 8(2), 41-56.

Akpan, P.O. and Undie, C.T., (2007). Investigating students' dropout in the university. *Journal of Educational Research*. 2 (1), 23-31.

Arowolo, D. E., & Ogunboyede, K., (2013). Confronting Governance Challenges in the Nigerian Universities within the Context of Failing Economy. *International Journal of Learning and Development*, 3(1), 138-147.

Ausburn, L. J. & Ausburn, F.B., (2004). *Desktop virtual reality: A powerful new technology for teaching and research in industrial teacher education*. London: Pearman.

Ajayi, I. A., & Haastrup, E.T., (2008). Management of University Education in Nigeria: Problems and Possible Solutions. *Revitalization of African Higher Education*, 4, 222-235.

Baruch, Y., & Lavi-Steiner, O., (2015). The career impact of management education from an average-ranked university: Human capital perspective. *Career Development International*, 20(3), 218-237.

Becker, S.O., Cinnirella, F., & Woessmann, L., (2012). The effect of investment in children's education on fertility in 1816 Prussia. *Cliometrica*, 6(1), 29-44.

Bello, T. O. (2012). Funding for Research in Science and Technology in Nigeria Universities: The Gender Perspective. *Journal of Emerging Trends in Educational Research and Policy Studies*, 3(1), 34-38.

Cardarelli, F. (2008). *Materials handbook: a concise desktop reference*. London: Springer Science & Business Media.

Chukwurah, C. C. (2011). Access to higher education in Nigeria: The University of Calabar at a glance. *Canadian Social Science*, 7(3), 3-15.

Clark, N. (2013). *Education in Nigeria*. World Education News & Reviews. Retrieved from *library.usask.ca/find/ejournals/view* on 15th Feb., 2017.

Cohen, L., Manion, L. & Morrison, K., (2013). *Research methods in education*. New York: Routledge.

Coleman, J.S. (2015). *Education and Political Development.* (4).Princeton: University Press.

de La Fuente, A. (2011). Human capital and productivity. *Nordic Economic Policy Review*, 2(2), 103-132.

Kanyip, B.P. (2013). Admission Crisis in Nigerian Universities: The Challenges Youth and Parents Face in Seeking Admission. *PhD dissertation presented to the Seton Hall University.*

Khan, M.T. (2014). Effects of Education and Training on Human Capital - And Effects of

Human Capital on Economic Activity (A Literature Based Research). *International Journal of Information, Business and Management*, 6(3), 90-102.

KPMG. (2014). *Nigeria's Oil and Gas Industry Brief.* Lagos: KPMG International.

Lulat, Y.G.M. (2005). *A History of African Higher Education from Antiquity to the Present A Critical Synthesis.* Westport: Praeger Publishers.

Matthew, D., Joro, I.D. & Manasseh, H., (2015). The Role of Information Communication

Technology in Nigeria's Educational System. *International Journal*, 64 (1), 25-37.

Moti U. G. (2010). The challenges of access to university education in Nigeria. *DSM Business Review*, 2, (2), 8-14.

Myers, M.D. (2013). *Qualitative research in business and management.* London: Sage.

National Bureau of Statistics. (2016). *Man-power production from universities.* Abuja: Government Publishers.

National Policy of Education. (2004). *Federal Government of Nigeria.* Lagos: Government Publishers.

National Universities Commission. (2016). *Federal Government of Nigeria.* Abuja: Government Publishers.

National Universities Commission. (2015). *Federal Government of Nigeria.* Abuja: Government Publishers.

Nevin, A.S., Akinbiyi, A. & Nwokoneya, Q., (2016). *Nigeria 2016 Q1 GDP: Economy contracts to -0.36%oy/y*. Economy Alert. Lagos: PWC Nigeria.

Nigerian National Petroleum Corporation. (2015). *Annual Statistical 2015 Bulletin*. Retrieved from *nnpcgroup.com* on 12 Nov., 2016.

Nyewusira, B.N. (2014). *A Historical Appraisal of the Aftermath of Politics on Autonomy and Control in Nigerian University Education: The Case of National Universities Commission*. Ibadan: University Press.

Ocholla, D.N. (2003). An overview of information and communication technologies (ICT) in the LIS schools of Eastern and Southern Africa. *Education for information, 21*(2 & 3), 181-194.

Odebode, S.O. (2014). Appropriate technology for cassava processing in Nigeria: User's point of view. *Journal of International Women's Studies, 9*(3), 269-286.

Okorafor, A.O. (2014). Developing Indigenous Technology for Harnessing Local Natural Resources in Nigeria: The Place of Technical Vocational Education and Training. *International Journal of Science and Technology, 3*(8), 12-24.

Okebukola, P. (2006). Principles and policies guiding current reforms in Nigerian universities. *Journal of Higher Education in Africa/ Revue de l'enseignement supérieur en Afrique*, 5, 25-36.

Okoroma N. S. (2008). Admission policies and the quality of university education in Nigeria. *Educational Research Quarterly*, 31, 22-36.

Olaniyan, D.A., & Okemakinde, T., (2008). Human Capital Theory: Implications for Educational Development. *European Journal of Scientific Research* 24, (2), 157-162.

Onokerhorage, P. (2000) "Crises Management in Nigeria Universities," *University system*, A quarterly publication of the National Universities Commission, Abuja, 10, (3), 12-25.

Oyedepo, S. O. (2014). Towards achieving energy for sustainable development in Nigeria. *Renewable and Sustainable Energy Reviews*, 34, 255-272.

Saunders, M., Lewis, P., & Thornhill, A., (2012). *Research Methods for Business Students* (6th Ed.). London: Pearson Education.

Silverman, D. (2016). *Qualitative research*. New York: Sage.

Tuckman, B.W. & Harper, B.E., (2012). *Conducting educational research*. London: Rowman and Littlefield.

Ugwuanyi, G.O. (2014). Taxation and Tertiary Education Enhancement in Nigeria: An Evaluation of the Education Tax Fund (ETF) Between 1999-2010.

Uwaifo, V.O. (2009). Technical education and its challenges in Nigeria in the 21st Century. *International NGO Journal.* 5, (2), 40-44.

Weed, M. (2008). Meta-interpretation a method for the interpretive synthesis of qualitative research. *Forum: Qualitative Social Research* 6: Art 37.

Zhu, C. (2012). Student Satisfaction, Performance, and Knowledge Construction in Online Collaborative Learning. *Educational Technology & Society, 15*(1), 127-136.

Chapter 10

Conclusion: Envisioning technology driven curriculum in African Higher Education: Ubuntu Perspective

Sekitla Daniel Makhasane
&
Lawrence Meda

Introduction

In this concluding chapter, we reflect on the main issues discussed in the book. The reflection is done from a perspective that adds an African world view flavour to the book. In other words, we locate our reflections in a postcolonial indigenous paradigm with the focus on Africa since the book is based on the findings from selected African countries. Our understanding of such a paradigm is influenced by Chilisa (2012, p. 20) who claims:

> A postcolonial indigenous research paradigm articulates the shared aspects of ontology, epistemology, axiology, and research methodologies of the colonised Other discussed by scholars who conduct research in former colonised societies in Africa, Asia, and Latin America; among indigenous peoples in Australia, Canada, the United States, and other parts of the world, and among the disempowered, historically marginalised social groups that encounter the colonising effect of Eurocentric research paradigms.

The postcolonial indigenous research paradigm can be used to respond to a call pertaining to Afrocentric education system in African universities where African ways of knowing into teaching and learning are given prominence. Nkoane (2006) contends that Afrocentric education is concerned with describing, interpreting, encouraging and transmitting African philosophy, thought, culture and identity. Debates for Afrocentric education system existed in literature for several decades with little progress on implementing suggested theories (Nkoane, 2006).

While there are ongoing debates about Afrocentric education system in African institutions of higher learning, it seems that little is known about African ways of knowing (Ngara, 2012). This chapter, therefore, concludes the book and contributes to the debates pertaining to African ways of knowing with specific focus on curriculum driven by technology in selected African universities. The first section discusses African philosophy of Ubuntu. This is followed by the infusion of central findings of book chapters to the African standpoint of Ubuntu.

Understanding Ubuntu as an African philosophical foundation

Given this book's focus on seeking to understand technology driven curriculum in selected African countries, it was appropriate to adopt Ubuntu philosophy as the frame for understand and making meaning of the main issues which emerged from the chapters. As observed by Mentz and Xaba (2013, p. 62) "…Ubuntu … is a philosophical concept that permeates all African life". While we are cautious about treating African countries and their people as homogenous, we argue that the Ubuntu approach is applicable in many African countries.

Ubuntu is an isiZulu (Language spoken by the Zulu people of the Republic of South Africa) word that means "humanness" (Mentz and Xaba, 2013). Words with similar meanings are also found in other African languages. For example, in Sesotho (Lesotho and South African language) it is called *botho*. Jimu (2016) provides examples from other African countries as follows: *hunhu* is a Shona (Zimbabwe) word, *Botho* is spoken in Botswana while *bumuntu* is used in Tanzania. Jimu (2016) further states that these words *bomoto*, *gimuntu*, *umunthu*, *vumuntu* and *umuntu* are used in Congo, Angola, Malawi, Mozambique and Uganda respectively.

Nussbaum (2003, p.2) defines Ubuntu as "…the capacity in African culture to express compassion, reciprocity, dignity, harmony and humanity in the interests of building and maintaining community with justice and mutual caring". The essence of Ubuntu is captured in the African proverb *umuntu ngumuntu ngabantu* (Mentz & Xaba, 2013). This African proverb depicts a philosophical meaning of Ubuntu which implies, inter alia, caring, respect, sharing and dignity.

Ubuntu finds its most lucid expression in the communal African way of life (Letseka, 2016). This communalism is characterised, inter alia, by such values as group solidarity, teamwork, respect for others and service to others with the understanding that people are interdependent (Mbigi, 2005). Ubuntu is rooted in the belief that community support leads to community strength. To this effect, identity and dignity can be realised through community commitment, empathy, mutualism and generosity (Swanson, 2012).

The communal and extended family system values promote African moral social order. These values prevailed in the way in which traditional African societies organised themselves. In such societies, an individual's issues also concern his/her nuclear family and extended family as well as the entire village. Given this communal approach, any problems could be solved by the society. This approach is still pertinent in today's African society (Muleya, 2016) since Africans identify themselves as members of the community (Abubakar, 2011).

The conceptualisation of Ubuntu portrays African way of life. It privileges communalism over individualism. In other words, an individual's importance is seen or observed in relation to the community. This way of life can be found in any organisation such as the university. The conceptualisation of Ubuntu as an integral component of success in the African context is used as a framework to view central findings of chapters that make this book.

Ubuntu and central themes emerging from the chapters

This section is organised into four themes which emerged from the chapters in this book: i) Collaboration and cooperative learning using technology; ii) Embracing of technology by universities; iii) Intersection between academic and non-academic use of technology, and iv) Challenges of using technology in African universities.

i) Collaboration and cooperative learning using technology

The use of technology is of paramount importance in bringing the spatial divide among students. It acts as a tool that enables collaboration among students. Collaboration is one of the fundamental principles of Ubuntu. As the African Saying goes *Motho ke motho ka batho* or *umuntu ngubuntu ngabantu* - which both means a person is considered human because of his relationship with other humans. Students in African universities shape their identities and abilities to succeed in learning through other students. The idea of collaboration highlights the interdependence of students in the process of teaching and learning.

Collaboration, sharing and extending a helping hand to others are not foreign actions to African students. This notion manifested through students' sharing of technological devices and collaboratively working together for a common goal. The aspect of sharing and collaboration are inborn among African children. Their parents have those virtues and they transfer them to their children by engaging them into the philosophy of Ubuntu from early ages. Mawere (2013) concurs that indigenous knowledge which is Ubuntu laden is transferred from one generation to another. The use of technology has improved interactions among students since they can share information regardless of their geographical locations. Emerging technologies such as WhatsApp, Facebook and Twitter are used by students to exchange ideas and engage into meaningful academic discussions. Students are using technology to learn by scaffolding one another which is a strong element of the African philosophy of Ubuntu.

ii) Embracing of technology by universities

All the chapters in this book highlighted the notion that institutions of Higher Learning in African countries have integrated technology into teaching and learning. Lecturers and students are moving with time. The 21st century has witnessed high demand of higher education in African countries. This massification of education has placed huge challenges on universities to ensure that many students have access to quality higher education. To this effect, even the traditional universities use technology to offer tuition through distance learning to students who cannot study full-time. The embracing of technology in African universities extends the philosophy of Ubuntu as higher education institutions are viewed as global villages (Meda, 2016) where students from all countries in the world can interact and share educational resources. Embracing of technology in African universities is making it possible for students to engage with their educational tasks with easy as resources are available and the quality of teaching and learning are modern.

iii) Intersection between academic and non-academic use of technology

As indicated earlier in this chapter, the studied universities promoted the use of technology by lecturers and students. The students used technology devices provided by the universities and their own. There was an intersection on the usage of technology where students used it for academic and non-academic purposes. The use of social media such as WhatsApp, Facebook and Twitter were predominantly for non-academic purposes although some academics utilised them as effective platforms for interactive and experiential learning.

iv) The challenges of using technology in universities

Despite a great interest in the use of digital technologies, African universities which were investigated seemed to have similar challenges to maximisation of ICTs in teaching and learning. The challenges include shortage of computers, poor internet connectivity and lack of funding to buy data bundles and smart phones. Although there is noticeable desire and a will to maximise the integration of technology into learning, many African universities are faced with challenges. It is interesting to note that, regardless of a myriad of challenges to integrating technology in African universities, academics and students are walking the talk. Rambe (2017) postulates that technology in African universities is being used optimally to provide spaces for interactive engagement. He reiterates that the use of Google groups enhances collaborative learning among students in South African Universities.

Similarly, Rambe and Bere (2013) state that emerging technologies such as mobile instant messaging are used in African universities to leverage students' participation and transform pedagogy. Higher education sector in Africa is forced to use educational technology to keep up with needs of a 21st century student (Bozalek, Gachago and Watters 2015). Placing computers in the classroom is not adequate enough for students to be competitive in the new millennium. There is a need for academics to integrate technology in a way that promote interaction and collaboration. This resonates with the African philosophical underpinning of Ubuntu which require elements of sharing, collaboration and partnership to be mainstreamed.

The challenges such as shortage of computers and limited internet connectivity implies that at any given time some students are able to use computers while others have to wait for their turn. However, students manage to mitigate these challenges through the use of their personal laptops and sharing with those who do not own such devices. Muleya (2016) argues that the communal and family system values of Ubuntu position an individual's problem as a concern for the community at large. In this case, the problem of students who do not have laptops, is a concern for some members of the university community especially friends. That is why they overcome the problem collectively by sharing the little that they have so that success will not be defined from an individualistic point of view, but communal.

Final word

Central themes which came out from chapters in this book were categorised into four: i) Collaboration and cooperative learning using technology; ii) Embracing of technology by universities; iii) Intersection between academic and non-academic use of technology, and iv) Challenges of using technology in African universities. The themes were analysed using the African philosophical understanding of Ubuntu. It is concluded that although African universities face challenges which prevent them from maximising the integration of technology into higher education learning, the continent's philosophical underpinning of Ubuntu makes teaching and learning more effective. Students share and collaborate in different spaces and that makes it possible for effective learning to take place in a context where technological gadgets are scare.

References

Abubakar, A. A. (2011). Proverbs as sources of philosophical ideas about African education.
In A. B. Nsamenang & T. M. S. Tchombe (eds.), *Handbook of African educational theories and practices: a generative teacher education curriculum.* Bamenda, Cameroon: Human Resource Centre.
Bozalek, V., Gachago, D. & Watters, K. (2015). Twenty-first-century pedagogies: portraits of South African higher educators using emerging technologies. In: V Bozalek, D Ng'ambi, D Wood, J Herrington, J Hardman and A. Amory (Eds.). *Activity Theory, Authentic Learning and Emerging Technologies: Towards a transformative higher education pedagogy* (Pp. 115-125). London: Routledge.
Chilisa, B. (2012). *Indigenous research methodologies.* Los Angeles: SAGE Publications Ltd.
Jimu, I. M. (2016). Shared sociability and humanity. *Africology: the Journal of Pan African Studies,* 9 (4), 404-411.
Letseka, M. (2016). Introduction: open distance learning (ODL) and the philosophy of ubuntu. In M. Letseka (ed.) *Open distance learning (ODL) through the philosophy of ubuntu* (1-16). New York: Nova Publishers.
Mawere, M. (2013). Rethinking the epistemological divide between science and other knowledge forms in environmental studies: an anthropological review. *The International Journal of Humanities & Social Studies,* 1 (2), 1-6.
Meda, L. (2016). Are we helping them to pass or setting them up for failure? Assessment related experiences of partially sighted students. *Journal of Communication,* 7(1), 43-52.
Mentz, P.J., & Xaba, M. I. (2013). Perspectives on the school as an organisation. In P.C. van der Westhuizen (Ed.), *Schools as organisations* (4ed., pp. 34-80). Pretoria: Van Schaik Publishers.

Mbigi, L. (2005). *The spirit of African leadership*. Randburg: Knowledge Resources.

Muleya, G. (2016). Managing and leading through ubuntu. In M. Letseka (ed.), *Open distance learning (ODL) through the philosophy of ubuntu* (pp. 185-197). New York: Nova.

Ngara, C. (2012). African ways of knowing: rethinking pedagogy in Africa. In H. K. Wright & A. A. Abdi (eds.,), *The dialectics of African education and western discourses: counter-hegemonic perspectives* (PP. 129-147). New York: Peter Lung Publishing.

Nkoane, M. M. (2006). The Africanisation of university in Africa. *Alternation*, 13(1), 49-69.

Nussbaum, B. (2003). African culture and ubuntu: reflections of a South African in America. *Perspectives*, 17 (1), 1-12.

Rambe, P. (2017). Spaces for interactive engagement or technology for differential academic participation? Google Groups for collaborative learning at a South African University. *J Comput High Educ*, DOI 10.1007/s12528-017-9141-5

Rambe, P., & Bere, A. (2013). Using mobile instant messaging to leverage learner participation and transform pedagogy at a South African University of Technology, *British Journal of Educational Technology*, 44(4), 544–561.

Swanson, D. (2012). Ubuntu, African epistemology and development: contributions contradictions, tensions, and possibilities. In H. K. Wright & A. A. Abdi (eds.,), *The dialectics of African education and western discourses: counter-hegemonic perspectives* (pp. 27-52). New York: Peter Lung Publishing.

www.ingramcontent.com/pod-product-compliance
Lightning Source LLC
Chambersburg PA
CBHW071204240426
43668CB00032B/2072